Ranches

of the American West

Ranches

of the American West

LINDA LEIGH PAUL

Principal Photography by Michael Mathers

RIZZOLI
NEW YORK

First published in the United States of America in 2009
by Rizzoli International Publications, Inc.
300 Park Avenue South
New York, NY 10010
www.rizzoliusa.com

2009 2010 2011 2012 / 10 9 8 7 6 5 4 3 2 1

Printed in China

Design by Lynne Yeamans

ISBN-13: 978-0-8478-3248-4

Library of Congress Control Number: 2009924415

PHOTOGRAPHY CREDITS

Courtesy *Veranda* magazine, photograph by Peter Vitale: 2–3, 168 (bottom left), 171, 173, 174

© Darrell Gulin/CORBIS: 4

Courtesy Palace of the Governors (MNM/DCA), photograph by Thomas Fitzsimmons, ca. 1906: 6–7

© Richard Cummins/CORBIS: 10–11

Courtesy Palace of the Governors (MNM/DCA), photography by Thomas Fitzsimmons, ca. 1915: 12, 13

Photographer unknown: 15

Yellowstone Art Museum Permanent Collection, Gift of Virginia Snook. Reprinted with permission of Will James Art Co., Billings, MT. 406.656.2851: 165 (left)

Norman Arnold: 187, 188, 189 (left)

Jim Bartsch: 234–35, 256–64

Gordon Gregory: 35, 60, 62 (upper right), 65, 67, 68–69, 92, 96 (lower left), 100–02

Michael Mathers: 5, 18–27, 28–34, 36–47, 48, 50–51, 53, 54 (right), 56, 61, 62 (left, lower right), 63, 64, 66, 70–77, 78, 81, 84, 86, 87 (right), 93–95, 96 (upper left, right), 98, 103, 104–31, 134–35, 138, 140–43, 146 (left), 149, 154–64, 165 (right), 166–67, 168 (top), 169–70, 172, 175, 176–85, 186, 189 (right), 190–91, 194–202, 203 (lower left and right), 204–09, 212–33, 246–55, 266–75

Jack Parsons: 192, 193

Kevin Perrenoud: 144–45, 146 (right), 147–48, 150–51

Magnus Stark: 79, 80, 82, 83, 85, 87 (left), 88–91

Timothy Street-Porter: 278–87

Pat Sudmeier: 132, 133, 136–37, 139

Roger Wade: 49, 52, 54, 55, 57–59, 61, 66, 68, 71

PREVIOUS PAGES: A new building is part of the restoration of a precious historic south Texas ranch. The architect was Don B. McDonald.

ABOVE: A band of cowboys, Seneca, Oregon.

OPPOSITE: A staircase from an old farmhouse.

ABOVE: Captain French's home on the Vermejo, Colfax County, New Mexico, circa 1906. The veranda wrapped around the large, French prairie–style house; the stone building was food storage. The tower in the center was used as protection against marauders. The barn at the back left was of the archetypical "dogtrot" style: two barns with a space in between.

CONTENTS

Cape Lookout
Trevittstown
YAM HILL
La Fayette
PORTLAND
Milwaukie
Oregon City
Mt Hood
CLACKAMAS
Parkersville
Salt Cr.
L. La Bish
Dallas
City
SALEM
POLK
MARION
WASCO
Des Chutes R.
C. Foulweather
Santiam City
Abiqua Bay
Syracuse
N. Santiam R.
Mt Jefferson
Corvallis
Albany
St Marys Peak
Mt Snelling
Washington Butte
BENTON
LINN
Stacy P.
Union Pt.
S. Santiam R.
Calapooya R.
Sinslaw R.
McKenzies Fork
Eugene City
Spencers Butte
Middle Fork
Umpqua City
Gardiner
UMPQUA
Fremont's Route 1843
East Fork
Umpqua Head
Calapooya Mts.
LANE
Providence
Scottsburg
Middletown
Elkton
Myrtle City
Coos R.
Coos R.
Fall Cr.
Ft. of Willamette
S. Calapooya R.
East Fork
C. Arago
Empire City
Winchester
West Fork
E
Randolph
N. Umpqua R.
COOS
DOUGLAS
KLAMATH
Roseburg
Canonville
So Umpqua
O
R
Port Orford
Con. Cr.
Klamath L.
Rogue R.
Summer
UTUAM
JOSE
JACK
Kerbyville
Rogue R.
SON
CURRY
Illinois R.
Lane
Mt Pitt
PINE
Ambrose
Jacksonville
Stewarts Cr.
Klamath L.
Wall...
Althouse
Mts.

Part I

If we could observe in slow motion the evolution of ranches, each in its terrain, we would see that the mountains, mesas, canyons, and plains are the shapes that inspire the architecture.

Introduction

The fashioning of ranches in the West began as a meandering and convoluted journey. In a trail of movement and flux, a story of literal mountains of obstacles, settlers used their immigrant's strength and courage to claim their pieces of land. Ranches were an afterthought; comfort was not a part of life for men moving wild cattle and horses on their journeys through the uninhabited and unambiguous West. Cattle was moving north, prospectors and pioneers were moving west, horses wandered over the mountains toward the coast, and sheep moved into the mountains and valleys.

The territories were larger than the men's imaginations, defining the need for outstanding horsemen, or as we have come to know them, cowboys. In a declaration it was said, "To the Mexicans the American cowboy owed his vocation. For his character he was indebted to no one." It was true, the cowboys and their character governed the western range.

The cowboys, however, were not ranch owners. They slept in bunkhouses, line camps, and under their horses when on the trail. A ranch was never a house. It was land—range and grazing, rivers and streams—defined only by the number of cattle that roamed it. Hay barns, stalls, corrals, calving sheds, and wagon sheds were built where they were needed, near a cookhouse or a small cabin. The development of ranch living quarters was modest. Ranch houses grew not from design, but as writer Tom McGuane points out, "from an improvisatory nature" over time (his own office was once a bunkhouse). And as in ancient Rome, when one building fell, its usable components were gathered and used again in new structures.

The northern climates were an enormous challenge. High elevation, long winters, deep snow, and mud were offset by the wildflower colors and warm sun that arrived in late summer. When the Scottish, English, and French came to the mountains north of the Great Plains, the year-round evergreens and summer valleys provided resources for their homes. The harsh winters required sturdy, functional shelters. With piers for supporting large wood posts and beams, the houses were strong enough to last several generations or longer. Logs and timber were assembled to accommodate rooflines that followed the configurations of the mountains. Small windows and large fireplaces were fundamental to the demands of the climate. When necessity called for more space, the "improvisatory nature" of northern buildings meant adding a second level above the fireplaces below. The rising warmth of the lower levels heated the new rooms. The Shining Mountain Ranch in Montana is an example of the rustic post-and-beam design used in its essence to create a contemporary working ranch complex.

LEFT: Texas bluebonnets cover a field surrounding an old farmhouse in the Central Texas Hill Country.

New Mexico is well known for its architectural origins rooted in the Anasazi constructs and Spanish building influences. However, the high desert regions of northern New Mexico had different resources, producing a different architecture. Rocks and stone used in construction were reddish-brown in color, invoking the name "Vermejo." The northern red and English oaks, ponderosa pine, and Douglas firs native to the southern Rocky Mountains, from northwest Wyoming to Santa Fe, resulted in a heavy, wilderness-lodge–style construction. On every hillside in the mountainous forests and high deserts, building materials were available for intricate ceiling designs, squared beams, flooring, and door and window framing. In form and style the architecture, as seen in the Vermejo Park Ranch's main house, Casa

Grande, was influenced by Spanish loggias, bell towers, mission-style facades, arches, and corridors to create a low-slung, hacienda "groundscaper" tucked horizontally into the foothills.

Architecture changes dramatically as one moves south. In New Mexico the climate and history become more conspicuous. The most apparent change is in the type of materials used; the second is the use of straight lines. The convergence of ancient Anasazi techniques of construction, level lines, and geometric volumes with the absence of hallways and the Spanish preference for softer, rounder surfaces, long exterior *corrédors*, porches, and courtyards resulted in a highly refined, yet suggestively primitive form. Cut stones, sticks and saplings, handmade bricks, and plaster were the

ABOVE: The home of W. H. Bartlett, Vermejo Park Ranch, New Mexico, circa 1915. *Casa Grande*, the house of Bartlett, Jr., is on the left; Norman W. Bartlett's house is in the center, and W. H. Bartlett's house is on the right.

OPPOSITE ABOVE: The living hall, W. H. Bartlett house, Vermejo Park, New Mexico, circa 1915.

OPPOSITE BELOW: The loggia, W. H. Bartlett house, Vermejo Park, New Mexico, circa 1915.

materials of the new indigenous architecture. The thickness of walls and placement of windows moderated temperatures. Handmade tiles became the thermal governor of the climate, cooling and storing heat as needed. Lacking glass or air-conditioning, it was pure architecture at its most sustainable.

Spanish and Mexican contributions to Texas architecture were expressive and meaningful. The earliest of the thirty-five Spanish mission buildings erected in the Texas territory were made of *gradd*, a mixture of brush, straw, and mud, and were similar in design to the *enramadas* or mission shelters, which were used as temporary housing while larger stone missions were under construction. The missions consisted of a stone chapel with special rooms, offices, dining areas, kitchens, and pantries for the priests and soldiers who lived there. Stones and other materials from the ruins of the early missions were used to build new structures in the mid-1800s.

The Spanish, however, weren't the only culture with an influence on the architecture of Texas. Germans flowed into Texas, as did the French, Irish, and English. Their legacy is the Texas adoration of limestone architecture. Texas limestone can be found in every significant building and ranch in the state. The fashion of handmade bricks and tile, or of cut limestone blocks and pavers, is an emblem of cultural elegance in the Texas architecture. Early forts such as the Cibolo Creek Ranch used a combination of stonework and adobe construction and a mix of historic architectural styles. Residential spaces were built to survive attacks in the territory. Family homes

such as the Gallagher Ranch were at times reduced to one building that was fortified against attacks— with high stone walls and windows or portholes that were only large enough for a gun to take outward aim.

When the Spanish settlers began to arrive in Alta, California, they came prepared to start new lives in an unknown place. They brought with them the items necessary for running a household and ranch and to enjoy the pleasures of the ranching life: trees to plant, seeds, cattle, household items, and the family linen. A few hundred Spanish ranches spread from San Diego to Sonoma. The ranches were built of adobe—straw and clay—similar to the Spanish mission architecture. Flooring, framing, and posts were made of wood; the roofs were tiled. The exteriors and interiors were plastered for protection against harsh coastal California weather. Stone, when available, was used for paths and fence posts.

Ranch architecture in California has changed little since the first *vaqueros* rounded up wild horses on the range there. The styles of the mid-1800s offered grace and economy. Spanish land grant holdings offered owners the opportunity to build historically significant ranch estates that would be held within families for generations. By the twentieth century, the new ranches of southern California were being designed and built by architects who admired the Spanish Colonial style. An early architect, Roy Seldon Price, was a master of emulation. Hollywood movie director Thomas H. Ince hired him to complete the ranch estate Dias Dorados. Henry W. Hall wrote in the *Pacific Coast Architect* in June 1924:

Mr. Roy Seldon Price . . . belongs to that class of designers who can be original without offending. . . . Early California architecture has been his inspiration. The ranch buildings are built of hollow tile, plaster and rock. . . . The low rooflines and road arches hark back to the simple spirit of the padres. The general crudity of the place is its greatest charm.[1]

Price's redesign of the Dias Dorados Ranch reveals a primitive yet refined approach to the low ranch layout. Variations on the master theme of a new Spanish Colonial Revival architecture made many architects wealthy and famous. John Byers and George Washington Smith are two of those architects whose work appears in this book.

North up the Pacific coast, the terrain in Oregon shifts from coastal mountains to inland valleys and arid desert lands. Southern and eastern Oregon is ranch land. Ranch architecture, until recently, has been early vernacular. The Oregon Basque community, founded by early sheep ranchers who migrated east from Nevada in 1880, erected ranch structures of sandstone. Earlier Klamath Basin tribal members used the rock and stone resources to build council houses and structures. Their constructs of rock and cedar were spiritual in nature. Architect Larry Pearson found the ritual of honoring materials in a commemorative way to be a compelling motivation when he was asked to create the Root Ranch in the Klamath basin. Based on the "rightness" of the material choices and appropriate technology, Pearson and the Roots have set the standard for the new American western ranch.

[1] Philip Ashton Rollins, *The Cowboy, An Unconventional History of Civilization on the Old-Time Cattle Range* (New York: C. Scribner's Sons, 1936), pp. 1, 186.

ABOVE LEFT: The arches and lattices of architect Roy Seldon Price's Dias Dorados Ranch, Southern California, 1925.

ABOVE: Simple irregularities and bulges enhance Price's primitive approach.

LEFT: The irregular edges of the arches and the paintings above the doors are a hallmark of the crudeness that has become known as architect Roy Seldon Price's "greatest charm."

MONTANA

GALLATIN

BEAVER HEAD

MADISON

JEFFERSON

EDGERTON

DEER LODGE

Benton
Swamp Creek
Arrow R.
Great Falls
Salt Lake
Gros Ventres
Judith
Kershey
Blackfoot Mission
Medicine R.
Smith R.
Yellow Water
Belt Mts.
Lieut. J. Mullan Road
Yellow Stone River
By
Yellow Stone
Cantonment Wright
Montana City
Gold
Labarge City
Gold
Hot Spring
Jefferson
Gallatin City
Bozeman
Big Boulder Cr.
Rosebud
Clark's Fork
Cantonment Stevens
Deer Lodge
Gold
Big Hole Pk. or Wisd.
Beaver Head
Bozeman City
Yellowstone R.
Gold
Gold
Hot Spring
Gold
Brandon
Stonewall
Gold
Sulphur Mt.
Hot Spring
Gold Mines
MADISON
Gold
Bannock City
Centreville
VIRGINIA CITY
McGallatin
Up. Yellow Stone L.
Falls
Stinking
Hot Spr.
Shell Cr.
Washington
Hot Spring
Yellow Stone L.
Crazy Woman
Crow Bull R.
Big Horn
Snake R.
Two Ocean Water
John Day Cr.
Camas Cr.
Three Forks
Market L.
Market Lake
Gold
Burnt Hole
Owl Cr.
SE
Pond d'Oreille Mission
Trading Post
Bitter Root R.
Gold
Fort Owen
LaBarge City
Gold
Hell Gate
Hot Spring

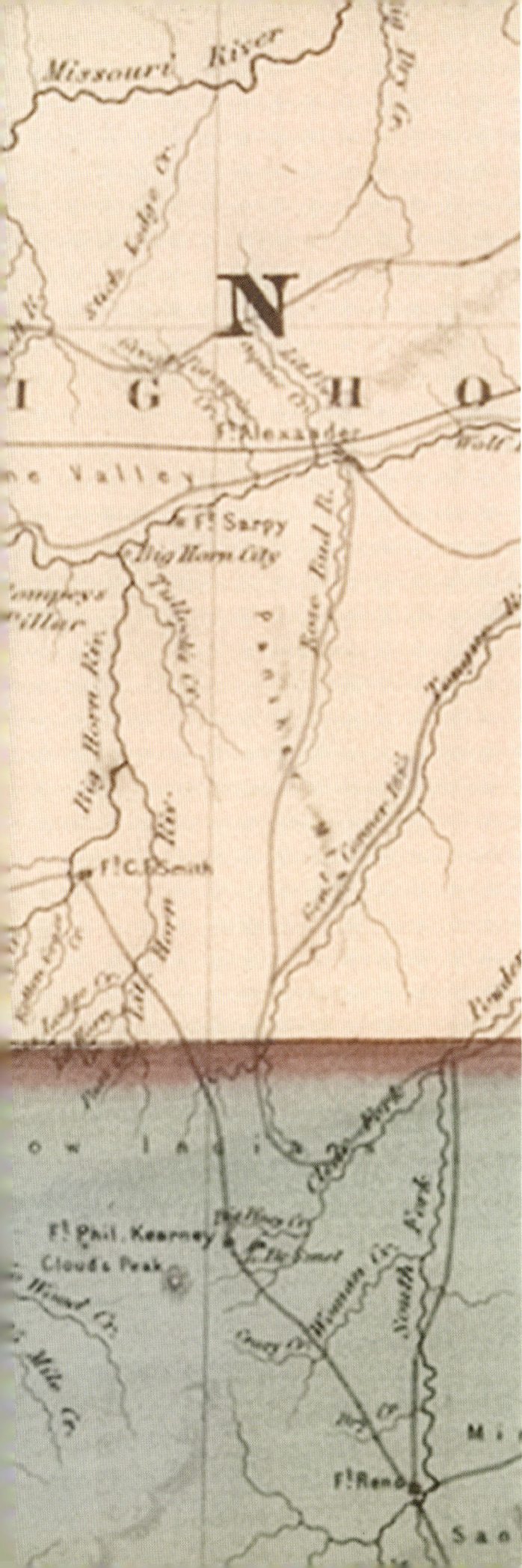

Part II: *The North*

Architectural influences in the northern territories began as early as circa 1790, when First Nation peoples (the Haida to the north and the Chinook to the south near the Columbia River) integrated a puzzle-based, interlocking system of architecture into their powerfully constructed buildings. These intricacies of design were learned in trades with Chinese sailors.

The Root Ranch, *Oregon*

Oregon's Klamath Basin, a place of immeasurable beauty and the site of the Root Ranch, is adjacent to ancient tribal communities. It is thought to be a powerful place: local Native Americans often undertook a spirit quest, which involved separation and a retreat to lonely spots; this valley is one of them. A legend of the ancient Klamath (the "encamped") people tells of two chiefs, Llao of the Below World and Skell of the Above World. The two were pitted in a powerful battle that resulted in the destruction of Llao's home 7,700 years ago; the battle was witnessed in the catastrophic eruption of Mount Mazama. The twelve-thousand-foot summit of the volcano collapsed and became a caldera filled with clear, frigid water to form Crater Lake. Located on the crest of the Cascade Mountain Range, it is one hundred miles east of the Pacific Ocean and stands as a totem at the end of the Klamath Valley, where the Klamath Native Americans revered the lake and the surrounding landscape.

For several years, Valerie and James Root looked for a spring-fed creek on ranch property. Their goal was not to simply build a home, but to find land with fishing potential and the opportunity to contribute to

LEFT: The moon above the Root Ranch in the Wood River Valley, south-central Oregon. The gathering room is on the left; the Council Room is on the right.

RIGHT: The gathering room was designed for views of Mt. Shasta and Crater Lake National Park in the distance.

stream restoration, the creation of spawning streams, the conversion of flood irrigation to beneficial stream flow use, and dry-land grazing. They successfully opened one additional full mile of spawning streams to expand resources for the needs of endangered fish. Fencing was installed along streams, creeks, and marshes to ensure limited impact on those delicate areas. The Roots also wanted to continue a cattle operation. To determine how best to use the land for their desired purposes, they worked hard and closely with the Klamath Tribes, the Klamath Basin Rangeland Trust, fish and wildlife agencies, other government agencies, and university research departments. The information they compiled in their research has been made public and is being used as a baseline for future projects.

The Root Ranch property is a confluence of spring-fed creeks and clear waters. The couple met

A B O V E : The French doors to the gathering room are flanked by unpeeled logs and a stone wall at the entry, reflecting the angle of the mountains. The outline of the Council Room is beyond.

O P P O S I T E : A century-old redwood salvaged from a five-foot-diameter Crater Lake water flume was treated and used in the ceiling. Unpeeled logs frame paned windows and rise to meet the redwood ceiling.

their architects, Larry Pearson and Adam Britt, while they were looking at houses in Montana that were built from recycled wood. The Roots wanted design plans of the style of an *estancia*—a South American cattle ranch—which would accommodate the active life of ranching, riding, fishing, entertaining, and running their businesses. *Estancia*-style architecture is also the essence of Argentina's history and culture. Valerie and James Root spent years traveling in Central and South America, especially Argentina. They gathered a significant collection of South American finds, including paintings by Milagros

Argüello and marvelous silver pieces, such as two late-eighteenth-century High Peru silver ornamental plaques from an alter or vaulted church niche. Matte chairs, antique wood tables, woven rugs, and a vast display of collected pieces would eventually be joined by commissioned iron lighting, recycled ancient redwood flumes, Oregon brownstone boulders, and the fine-spun garnishes of the French influence on 1930s Buenos Aires design.

Pearson was humbled by the basin landscape: the vastness of land, the distance of the valleys and mountains, the life forms. He knew the design must

LEFT: The Council Room features an Oregon stone fireplace and unique juniper tiles set in the sand floor.

OPPOSITE: The dining room adjacent to the foyer features a commissioned hand-forged iron chandelier and fireplace.

the radial form, the large central stone fireplace, and the stone wall. The wall begins at the main entry, follows a series of steps, then flows beside the steps into the living room. Along the western side of the house it travels out into the landscape. There it tapers to a soft, sloping angle into the terrain, gentle as the mountains in the distance. One side of the wall houses public spaces, such as the living room, and the other side offers sanctuary: bedroom, dressing room, and courtyard. A little window in the stone wall frames a pond and tree from the sanctuary side.

The Council Room is set deeper into the bench of land. The windows open through the grasses into the habitat. Fundamental rocks are tumbled against one another at the fireplace as if rolled down from the mountains. Large Oregon brownstone boulders form the base. Juniper logs are rough, not peaked, and placed in the vertical stack. The radial roof has a center truss. Faceted then vertical stacked logs create a plain window. A series of six to eight windows circumscribes the structure. The roof is hand-split, single shake.

For the floors, juniper wood was crafted into six-inch tiles, set with the end grain facing up. Sand was then swept into the spaces between the tiles, as mortar. A thin layer of lime was swept over the sand and sprinkled with water, forming a cementlike seal to set the juniper. The floor exudes a sense of the raw, naked earth.

be an extension of what he viewed: discreet, subtle, low to the terrain, and lodged into the slight hillside. Reading the site, he understood the panoramic nature of the valley floor. The early forms he envisioned were a circle and a line: a radial form intersected by a stone wall. But radial forms become prominent, and the Roots did not want the house to stand out. So the design adopted a horizontal nature, where the elevation is set six feet below the elevation of the "bench" landscape.

Pearson began working with the mastery he is known for: the "ranch" language.

The approach to the ranch is a half-mile-long drive across the bench land. The house is set slightly above a pond that is located at the intersection of two creeks. The two circular rooms are the living room, which has a view of the Southern Cascade Mountains and Pelican Peak ten to twelve miles across the valley floor, and the Council Room. The architect loved the creation of the tension between

LEFT: The gathering room at dusk with views over the pond to the mountains.

ABOVE: The leather furniture, draperies, and details from Peace Designs are brought together with the collections amid wood and stone materials.

Corral Creek Ranch, *Montana*

The Madison Valley in Montana is an original, natural landscape. Glacial routes created a convergence of three separate ecosystems: high timber mountains descend onto an unfurling of grassy hills that stretch to become flatlands filled with grazing pastures and wetlands.

The original 1940s Corral Creek ranch house sat on a protected site on the three-hundred-acre cattle operation. The new owners, Pam and Fred Rentschler, discovered the Madison Valley ranch after an extensive search in four states for an "end-of-the-road ranch." Their search criteria included the best fishing

and wildlife. Fred had wanted a ranch since the age of fourteen, when he spent a summer working on a cattle ranch in Wyoming. His vision of ranch life included hard work to maintain a working cattle ranch, control noxious weeds, restore the structures, tend alfalfa

BELOW: A horse in the pasture with the house and Madison Range in the distance.

RIGHT: A sitting area on the front porch. A stone path leads to a landscaped garden patio on the other side of the house.

crops, improve the fish habitat, and maintain hiking and horseback-riding trails. The owners had important design requirements to integrate their home with the needs of the land.

The Rentschlers selected their builder and contractor first. Harry Howard of Yellowstone Traditions recommended architect David Leavengood of Seattle for the Trapper's Line Cabin, the "soddy" pond-fishing cabin, and the guesthouse.

Larry Pearson of Livingston, Montana, provided his ranch expertise and deep knowledge of the west for the main house, the barn and tack room, the "show" house, and the chef's cabin. Decisions regarding special materials were made in a unique collaboration between builder, architect, owners, decorator Hilary Heminway, and stonemason Phil Cox. Dale Dombrowski designed the surrounding landscape, rock gardens, and stone walkways.

ABOVE: The front gate of the Corral Creek Ranch begins a long ride through pastures to the house at the base of the foothills.

UPPER RIGHT: The extensive front porch of flat-cut stone and Western red cedar emphasizes the open spaces and landscape surrounding the ranch.

LOWER RIGHT: A short stroll from the main house is this fishing cottage with a sod roof at the edge of the small lake.

The owner requirements stipulated that the renewed ranch house would save the original footprint of the former main house; also that parts of two fireplaces be incorporated into the new design. The goal was to pay homage to the previous owners, who are honored with dedicated monuments in the wilderness above the ranch. The new design is tucked into a low hill tree line where there is source water. The ranch is made up of the main lodge house and several buildings; a "line" cabin is accessible only by horseback. An entertainment cabin, a short walk from the house, offers a game room, bar, and screening room. Also on the property is a guest cabin, a small fishing cabin called a "soddy," and a spectacular barn that terminates with four upward tapering stone piers that bear the weight of a log hayloft above a drive-in storage bin.

The valley and hills roll out from the main house, which looks as though it has been a part of the landscape for a hundred years. Indigenous materials clad the exterior: unstained, unsealed, salvaged lodge-pole pine will be allowed to weather in the picturesque way of Montana fences and

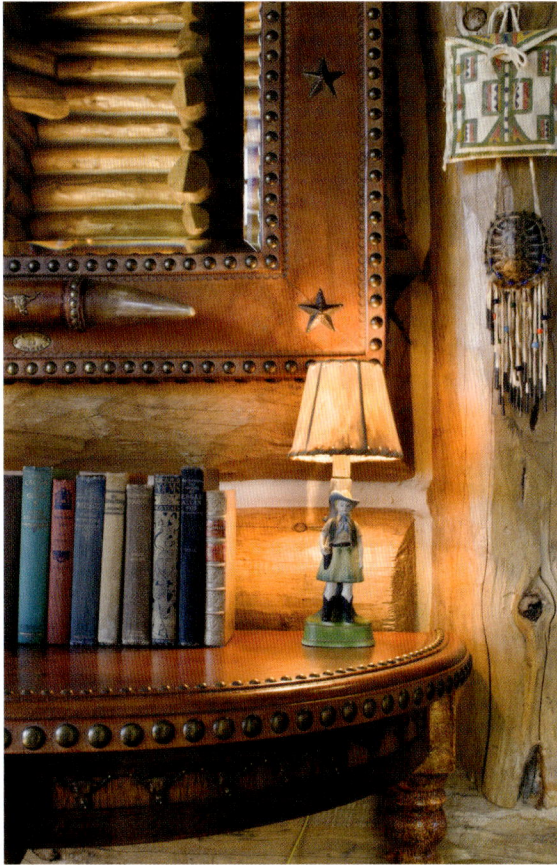

OPPOSITE: A view of the living area from the entry balcony. Peeled logs and varnished branches were designed to give balance to the western collections.

LEFT: A collection of western artifacts and Native American beadwork.

RIGHT: A Native American bone breastplate, a fringed and beaded leather tunic, a belt, amulets, and a skirt with silver medallions.

barns. Fieldstone, stacked throughout the home, was acquired from areas on the property, giving the building its sense of history. The highly textured bark of red cedar tree trunks supports beams and porches.

Designed to illustrate the history of the region, the interiors absorbed an extensive amount of material from the old ranch house. French antiques were surrendered in favor of custom pieces of beaming simplicity and grace. Locally harvested juniper and walnut were transformed by local artists into dramatic pieces, including writing desks, chairs, headboards for beds, and intricately perforated wood-slat or leather lampshades. Loft railings, bookshelves, staircase posts, and balusters were designed in geometric and freeform patterns in barked or pealed-and-sealed pine and cedar branches. An armoire and media, china, and crystal cabinets—made for special areas in living, dining, and bedrooms—are quietly integrated into the rooms. Antique Native American leather and bone breastplate, dress, and woven textiles occupy nooks and niches. Ancient woven baskets share vignettes with an antique Spanish-influenced leather-strap armchair and an old, western-style, stick-and-metal writing desk. Switchplates are of wrought iron. Beaded, stitched, and fringed chamois and heavy-grade leather sofas are steadfast against the roughness and ruggedness of ranch activities. The Rentschlers are avid collectors of works by western artists. "In many cases, we designed around a specific piece," says Heminway. However, the rooms are so well balanced that the rare bronze, painting, or artifact "doesn't scream at us to look at it."

Outside the many windows are natural wildlife corridors created by grizzly bears, wolves, elk, moose, pronghorn antelope, coyotes, and foxes. They graze on natural vegetation: timothy grasses and various range grasses, including bunch grass and needle grass, willows, aspen, cottonwood, creek bottom brushes, choke cherries, gooseberries, and currants. Occasionally the wildlife resorts to a domesticated alfalfa or patch of flowers. Flying above are bald eagles, hawks, falcons, kestrels, owls, sandhill cranes, blue heron, ducks, geese, and trumpeter swans. A chorus is created by the songs of the bluebirds and the western tanager.

LEFT: A bird's-eye view of the entry and living room with a reading nook and two sitting areas. The balcony leads to a small library and bedrooms.

ABOVE: A bedroom with custom twin beds and a floor lamp that features a bucking bronco.

LEFT: Each saddle, blanket, and bridle has its place in the tack room.

ABOVE TOP: Leather recliners furnish the vintage-style screening room.
Wood-paneled display walls and coffered ceilings evoke a historic movie house.

ABOVE BOTTOM: A log cabin outfitted for gaming with a pool table,
card table, screening room, outdoor deck, and full bar.

B Bar Ranch, *Montana*

The B Bar Ranch is the highest deeded land in the mountain-rimmed Tom Miner Basin, bordered by the Gallatin National Forest and Yellowstone National Park, a landscape shaped by glaciers and volcanoes, where the mountains are still growing and the rivers continue to cut through the geography. The B Bar was a homestead in the late 1880s and today is a working cattle ranch with a focus on rare breeds, heirloom crops, and livestock conservation. It sits among a diverse landscape and has a community of individuals of varied backgrounds who are all committed to preservation and the protection of nature.

Maryanne Mott began her relationship with Montana in 1973, when she visited the state to learn firsthand about the challenges that ranchers and native people were facing as a result of the coal strip mining there. Five years later, having supported numerous efforts to protect the land from mining operations, Maryanne and her late husband, Herman Warsh, began to look for a place of their own. They heard about the B Bar, and in February 1978, they rode

BELOW: At the edge of a trout pond on the ranch is a bronze moose by Doug Van Howd of Auburn, California.

RIGHT: The house known as "Triple Top" is set within the Tom Miner Basin, with Sheep Mountain looming in the background and Yellowstone beyond that.

snowmobiles over jack fences to get their first ground-level views of the ranch (the deep snows of that memorable winter of 1977–78 ruled out any other sort of access). The snow was almost to the eaves of the building, concealing a good share of the man-made improvements, but this mattered not to Maryanne and Herman, and the ranch became theirs.

Maryanne contacted architects Diana Marley and Sam Wells when considering the renovation of the existing lodge and asked them to design their home on the ranch. The house had to provide privacy for the owners in the middle of a public ranch setting. Maryanne wanted separation from the rest of the ranch while being able to watch over activities and join in as

she chose. The layout of the home, called Triple Top, is the solution to these requirements.

The site plan situated the buildings in close proximity to one another on the valley floor, rather than taking advantage of a multitude of dramatic hillside settings. The site selection protects the ranch

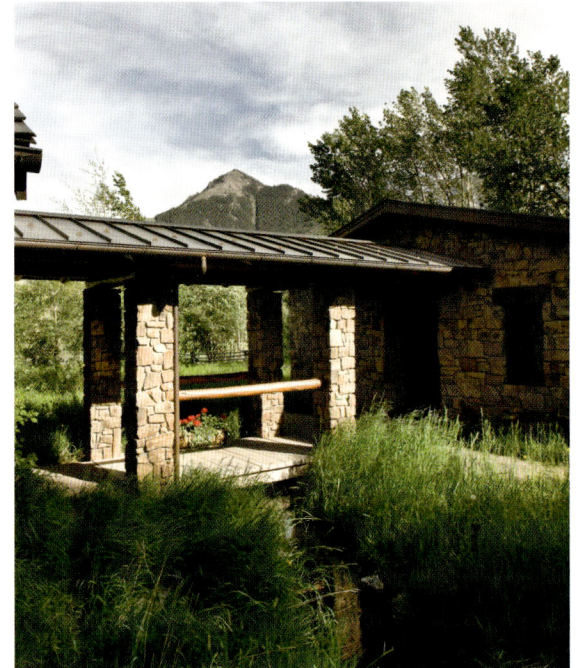

ABOVE: The ranch lodge is a headquarters for gatherings and festivities.

RIGHT: A copper-covered bridge over a creek links two buildings.

OPPOSITE: Triple Top from a private garden. The creek and bridge are on the left.

from what can be a harsh winter mountain environment. But Maryanne also believes that design should not disturb a splendid wilderness—one that even the architects believe rivals the beauty of nearby Yellowstone. Maryanne's love of the lands and her commitment to proper stewardship, practice of sustainability, and concern for habitat have all led her to ranch. Cabins and the remnants of the earlier ranchers that can still be seen on the property today are constant reminders of those practices.

The existing ranch is very rustic in nature: peeled log structures were built more than one hundred years ago. To respect the tradition in a meaningful way, the exterior design of the buildings shows the traditional peeled and chinked log appearance. The form and spacing, however, are modern in spirit. Rather than having exposed log work throughout the interior, troweled plaster in a buckskin tone was

utilized to subdue the visual effect of the jumbo logs. Other patterns of the past are carried forward wherever possible. Horse-drawn mowers are still used. But other methods of conservation required the use of appropriate new technology. For example, low-water, composting privies replace the old style.

Being practical, as a good ranch house should be, the house incorporates materials and features that by default make the design a thoroughly considered one in the context of today's world. The exterior stone, Eagle Moss rock, is local. Most of the wood was

LEFT: The draft horse barn at dawn.

BELOW: The herd of very tall Ancient White Parks showing their white coats and colored points: muzzles, ears, and feet. Their upswept lyre-shaped horns continue to twist as they age.

LEFT: Serving as a greenhouse for herbs, this porch connects the kitchen and living wing to the master bedroom wing.

BELOW: The entry foyer, with reclaimed wood from the ranch and floors of a copper-gray slate.

OPPOSITE: This is one of the enclosed porches that link the three buildings of Triple Top. Peeled and chinked log walls, peeled log rafters, and slate flooring create an "airlock" room to enter from the cold outdoors.

recently the settling of the area occurred." Riding horses through the hills, working the cattle, and walking the land are part of life here. Just when the family is ready to sit down for dinner the call comes to scramble down to the barn and assist with the birth of a new foal. It is hard work with long hours, but Maryanne, not a native Montanan, has earned her spurs. She has worked diligently to preserve and protect her piece of the West.

collected from nearby sources. The squared, heavy timbers came from a reclaimed mill. The oak floors are from a salvaged warehouse. The wood on the walls, cabinets, and doors was found in a dilapidated old homestead on the ranch. Every board was sanded and put to new use.

The interiors are furnished with a selection of pieces made for the ranch. The lodge living room features western paintings and bronzes. Furniture made by Don Hindman, a colleague of Thomas Molesworth, lends color and western form. A furniture-making "descendant" of Molesworth created

pieces for the bedroom. One of the most brilliant and enjoyable works of art is the bronze beaver sculpture that covers the fireplace opening. It is the creation of über-sculptor Kappy Wells of New Mexico. The sculpture is the visual focus of the sight line and serves a necessary function in creating a seal against the weather when the fireplace is not in use.

It is inspiring to peer into the remnants of one of the original cabins on the ranch. "It is hard to shake the sensation that those early pioneers were truly a breed apart," Maryanne says. "Coming upon a half-buried bison skull is a testament to how

LEFT: The view from the living room through the kitchen to the fireplace log storage and sitting area.

ABOVE: A hallway leads to the lodge dining room.

OPPOSITE, UPPER LEFT: The guest lodge living room furniture is by Don Hindman, a colleague of Molesworth. The elk sculpture is by Doug Van Howd.

OPPOSITE, LOWER LEFT: The bronze beaver sculpture that covers the fireplace when not in use is by Kappy Wells of New Mexico.

OPPOSITE, RIGHT: The den and library space in the office wing of Triple Top. A loft guest bedroom is above, where the Native American blankets hang over the railing.

Running Elk Ranch, *Montana*

Wild elk range, rest, and graze in newly restored ranch grasses. Upright on hind legs, males fight their rivals to win their choice of mates. Small herds of deer leap fences and cross dirt roads where the prairie meets the tree line up on the slopes of this rich western locale, just south of the snowcapped Bridger Mountains. This is the storied Gallatin Valley, abundant with habitat that supports the migration of Montana wildlife. Historical and picturesque sites of Ross Peak and Yellowstone National Park make up the nearby Rocky Mountain West.

The owner of the Running Elk Ranch, from a family of California ranchers, sought a home in the mountainous north to teach his own family a love of the wilderness. They wanted their Montana home to be at elevation, but not above six thousand feet. The property they landed was a three-thousand-acre former wheat field—the third-oldest ranch settled in the Gallatin Valley. The site fit their dedication to the land and became the family trust—a continuing

LEFT: The Running Elk guesthouse below the snow-capped Bridger Mountains in the Gallatin Valley.

BELOW: The massive timber main entry to the stunning ranch landscape.

homage to those first homesteaders of the Montana ranch and also to the owner's California ranch ancestry.

The adjacent ranches that were purchased to create Running Elk needed to be prepared for the site plan and construction. Two years were spent developing the hundreds of new acres needed. The owners required that the design for the property include a habitat for waterfowl, a trout hatchery, and water resources for personal recreation. Interconnecting streams throughout the ranch are part of the water design, created to fit the contours of the land.

Running Elk is a horse ranch. No livestock are on the property. It is a family retreat and has become an important part of the local community. The site has extensive property, and the ranch operation, like all ranches, is a collection of scattered buildings placed at appropriate locations to satisfy a number of design

PREVIOUS PAGES: The elk among the evergreens on the road to the arena.

OPPOSITE: The dining area and gallery in the horse arena.

RIGHT: The ranch manager, Mark Gustafson, is in the arena; his grandfather's saddle can be seen at the end of the gallery.

BELOW LEFT: The tack room and horse stalls.

BELOW RIGHT: The workroom and anvil where horseshoes are made.

requirements. The owners selected Locati Architects of Bozeman, Montana, for their vision of western architectural styling. A thirty-five-thousand-square-foot state-of-the-art arena with living quarters is at the forefront of the ranch activities and is one of the first structures to be seen upon the approach. An outdoor riding arena is nearby. One of two guesthouses, a barn, and a caretaker's house are close by; the main

house, a stone skeet-shooting house, a second guest-house, and several others are less apparent. The ranch manager, Mark Gustafson, a cowboy from a ranch family, has a splendid outfit to manage. A saddle at the gate to the arena floor belonged to Mark's grandfather. The indoor arena is built for practices, events, and shows. Running the length of the show floor is a bar-style gallery where guests may sit or stand with a beverage to watch the horse events. The arena is fitted with a professional kitchen for lunches and dinners.

Long, harvest-style tables fill the parallel space between the bar-railing gallery and the exterior window wall of the building. Under customized wrought-iron light fixtures, guests can view events in the riding ring while seated in the dining space. Also a part of the arena is a high-tech climbing wall. A bunkroom, stables, a tack room, and space where farriers work on anvils to forge shoes are all fitted with the tools of the trade. Local craftsmanship extends to every detail of the arena and horse care.

LEFT: The patio, fireplace, and dining area at the Spring Hill guesthouse.

ABOVE: The staircase shows the craftsmanship and handwork featured throughout the ranch.

OPPOSITE: The Spring Hill guesthouse patio is used for outdoor activities; in crisp weather it is heated.

LEFT: The living room has views of the Bridger Mountains.

OPPOSITE: The interior entry shows curved overhead beams and interior stonework.

The architectural intent of the Running Elk Ranch was to preserve the buildings that remained there when the land was bought. A wonderful example of this is the Spring Hill guesthouse. Built at one of the higher elevations on the ranch, the house exploited the remains of an archetypal ranch granary. High volumes, sloping rooflines, and large door openings fit in with the needs and requirements of the new cabin. Elements found on the property, such as stone and pieces of ranch architecture, were incorporated. The interior stone is a colorful local Montana rock quarried in the northwest part of the state. The architects chose to stack the stone in a manner that reflected the textures of rock faces and cliffs of the adjacent mountain ranges. The timber was selected for similar purposes. A major design feature is the signature curved trusses used by Locati Architects. The detailed truss frames create a gracious and spacious interior, while framing the iconic views. The dramatic feel of the interior causes the structural features to become less obtrusive, while creating a limitless feeling of space.

All the residences and buildings on the ranch were given the same level of attention. The owner requested that the ranch become a showcase for the rich pool of talented local craftspeople. Hardware was produced using an ancient process of sand casting; murals in glass pay homage to original wheat fields. Every room has an element or more that was crafted locally, commissioned to be the best expression of Montana's ranch aesthetic.

OPPOSITE: The living room, kitchen, and loft at the Spring Hill guesthouse.

ABOVE: The master bedroom with fireplace at the guesthouse.

Double D Homestead, *Montana*

The Double D Homestead is a Paint Horse ranch on an inactive placer gold mine, southwest of Bozeman in Madison County, Montana. After hiking the acreage of seventy or eighty ranch sites, Dick and Diana Beattie stumbled upon the Madison Valley ranch and began to buy up the old mining claims from the owner, who had originally purchased it for rock tailings and shipped rock off to Oregon. Eventually, the Beatties ended up with 750 acres, active with creeks, five ponds, some historic barns, and many smaller buildings. Three surrounding mountain ranges afford exquisite views. The main house is nestled in a Douglas fir forest commanding views toward the one-hundred-year-old sheep barns with rusted roofs, and beyond to the Big Sky Mountain. The Tobacco Root Mountains wrap behind the house, and the boulder-shaped Revenue Mountains climb toward the north.

The restoration of the ranch began with the owners' assurances that respect would be given to this historic property. They purchased a selection of century-old barns and buildings and made plans to have them moved to the ranch, where they were "restacked." First came three large 1890 barns, bought on a ten-degree-below-zero January day from Ted Turner's nearby Red Rock Ranch property. One barn was thirty by sixty feet and planned for use as a horse barn. The second barn, a twenty-four-by-thirty-six-foot structure, was designated to become the living room of the main house, which contained a small kitchen, a window-side dining area, a library,

LEFT: The rustic and elegant asymmetry of the front entrance to the Double D Homestead.

RIGHT: The restored Swedish guesthouse at the curve in the road, bordered by Montana Jack fencing.

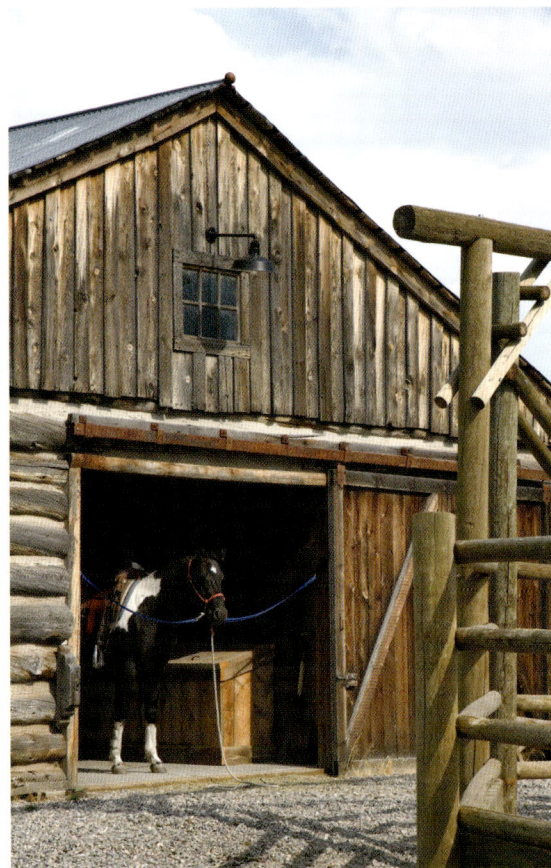

ABOVE: Diana's porch is a gathering place for family and guests.

ABOVE RIGHT: The stone and cedar bark–post fishing soddy is a relief from the late summer sun. Hop vines grow over the sapling-laden pergola-style roof.

RIGHT: The old barn with one of the Beatties' Tobiano Paints in the doorway.

OPPOSITE: A patio and fireplace for outdoor dining at the opposite side of the long, rustic porch.

and an open living room. Diana, herself a talented designer, wanted to have a formal dining room for entertaining, and this second barn was large enough to accommodate such a design arrangement.

A friend, David Laitinen, spent months making a front door, embellished with tiny twigs and featuring a stick man. Two stone corner fireplaces fit cozily into the small rooms, which house a master bedroom and dressing room both in the upstairs and main levels. On the main floor, the living, dining, and kitchen areas are well appointed with Swedish antiques of the nineteenth century.

A "dog trot"—a building of two equal barns under one roof with a space in the center for the dogs to trot through—functioned beautifully as two twenty-by-twenty-foot bedrooms: a guest bedroom and the master bedroom. Nearing completion of the project, architect Candace Miller was challenged with

the inclusion of an office for Dick. It was located just off the master bedroom and tucked into the landscape, so the view from the desk chair grazes over the tops of fescue grass to the valley. A radial entry stair descends into this exceptional space. Connecting the three structures is the stone structure that came from the mining excavation. The rounded rocks arrived with lichen growing on them, adding to the sense of elapsed time and the authenticity of the ranch. Stone and aged logs also set the tone. Reclaimed and restored materials were used as often as possible.

Candace used an architectural approach to govern the way she wanted the spaces to work in articulation to one another. The concept of compression and expansion was used repeatedly, such as in the small, cottagelike entry space, opening into the larger, unanticipated interior space, which grants a full and expansive view of the valley. The main living area has a taller, vaulted space, with bedrooms and a library that contract the scale back down to an appropriate volume. There are cozy spaces such as the grandchildren's nursery and an upstairs bedroom and office.

OPPOSITE: The interiors were done by Diana Beatie. Woven rugs and leather are accessorized with antique scales and a moose antler chandelier.

ABOVE LEFT: This custom branch-and-rod desk is perfectly scaled to fit the entry. The slender rods were made from fly-fishing rods, which add color and pattern to the piece. The delicate pieces and placement of the rods contrast with the logs and chinking backdrop.

ABOVE RIGHT: A patterned sideboard is the focal point for a vignette of Old West artifacts.

The Beatties had been living in their homestead building and entertaining their many family members and friends when they discovered they really needed a guesthouse. Laitinen, who was working with them on the horse barn, found an original Swedish homestead located deep in the Bridger Mountains. Unlike the three bold, timbered log buildings from Red Rock, this homestead, believed to have been built in 1886 and reworked in 1910–11, was in grave disrepair, nearly a complete loss. It stood at two stories and was about twenty-one by nineteen feet in size. The parts were restacked over a gold-mine ravine, and a lower level of stone was added. Rusted red corrugated tin was used for the roof as a historic tribute to the region. The guesthouse is one of the first buildings to be seen when approaching the property and houses two entire guest suites. The main floor and the lower level extend to the outdoors with porches and patios, to capture an expanded view of the main homestead, which stands a half-mile away. These outdoor areas are designed to ensure the house never becomes confining.

The outdoor space is, of course, as important on a ranch as the interior space. The extension of living outdoors with a covered porch that leads to an open patio, where activities engage the landscape, is essential. Montana *is* the great outdoors, and creating outdoor living spaces often results in several buildings in a number of select spots. Laitinen built a "garden shack" of stone and hewn timbers for daring children to camp out in. A trapper's cabin was moved to the ranch and converted into a playhouse. Reviewing a favorite historic encyclopedia of parks and recreation buildings, Diana found an Oklahoma pump house, which she had reproduced using boulder stones a few steps up from the pond that sits closest to the main house. The fishing cabin is a "soddy," with a roof of sod—a mix of wild grasses and wildflowers that sprout in June. The cabin provides relief from the ever-present summer sun, whether one is sitting on the porch, where the vines of hops wrap themselves around cedar bark-on posts, or inside, where in the cool stone surround there is a fireplace for winter sojourns.

ABOVE: The designer's sense of whimsy and love of color are evident in this guestroom. The scrolls of the wooden bed share a patina from the walls. The crewelwork on linen adds a period feel to the room.

OPPOSITE: The master bedroom has a classic four-poster bed and leather chairs.

McGuane Ranch, *Montana*

Author Tom's McGuane's first jaunt to the Northern Rockies was as a teenager in 1957, driving in a hotrod Chevy from his home state of Michigan, where the highest elevation is 1,979 feet. He especially remembers arriving in the Northern Rockies, experiencing the majesty of the mountains, the landscape of that breadth of scale, from which he claims he has never recovered. He recalls being a little worried about what he might be asked to do. He had never ridden a horse, and he knew that would be part of the experience. He had always been passionate about the natural world, but in the West, he recalls, that world seemed to be still in its original form. He was soon filled with the romance of the place. "I must have had some instinct about the importance of my experience at that time, as I have lived in the Northern Rockies since leaving school."

Today, Laurie and Tom McGuane ride horses to move cattle, to inspect stock water, fences, and springs, to deliver salt and minerals to their pastures, or just for pleasure. On harder days, they ride to

LEFT: The southwest Montana approach to the McGuane Ranch.

LEFT: The ranch house shows the rooflines and footprint of the original homestead. Eleven sets of wood-paned windows have been installed for more natural light.

ABOVE: The breakfast room and sunroom are at the opposite corner of the house.

train their horses for the roping or cutting cattle from the herds. In the past, they had a substantial herd of cows, bulls, and heifers, but they have recently simplified and converted to a yearling operation, which entails stocking rangeland in the spring; gathering and shipping in the fall. This supports the horse operation they now have, which includes the raising and training of cutting horses.

The McGuanes' ranch is the fourth one in a relatively small area noted for its beauty and balance of agricultural attributes. A pristine river runs past the corner of their house and through the middle of the ranch property. Their ranch buildings were all built by the original homesteader, an immigrant from Lancashire named George Muncaster. Many other homesteaders in the area were also from Lancashire. An English architectural historian verified the arrangement of home and outbuildings as typical of a Lancashire farmstead. The logs were cut in the forest miles away, floated down the river, hauled out, milled, and used to build the house and barn.

Tom points out that the improvisatory nature of the way ranches and their buildings grow over time often leaves little room for ranch design. For example, Tom's office was formerly in a bunkhouse, which was built similarly to the house and barn. Now his office is part library and research lab. The angled windows above the bookshelves are spaced below a clerestory-style ribbon of windows higher up on the wall. It is the consummate writer's refuge.

LEFT: The bright, two-story living room features a leaded-glass window above paned windows, facing the front lawn.

OPPOSITE: The main-level living room; the dining room to the right; and the loft above.

the window it replaced. Log houses are inclined to be dark, and a lot of the work Tom and Laurie have done addresses the issues of light. In the winter, light is critical. Two years ago, skylights were added in the living room. The play of light and shadow in the passing cloudscapes overhead adds another dimension to the interiors of the house. The goals for the interiors are to get yet more light inside and to create spaces for privacy and work.

Interiors are accessorized with objects from unlikely old stores, old diaries from secondhand stores, a relatively rare 1910 Maynard Dixon painting of a Montana scene, and another early Dixon painted on the Blackfeet Indian reservation. A third Dixon is from the period when the artist's work turned from the "old West" toward modernism; this one is a 1930s characteristic cloudscape. A watercolor of a thunderstorm is by Charles Burchfield; another work is by Russell Chatham. A Will James fingerpainting was done while he was in the Billings jail.

A landscape of mountain foothills, short-grass prairie, and juniper savannas provides the basic nourishment for livestock and indigenous animals. Buffalo grass, little bluestem, vetch, orchard grass, reedy canary, and timothy grasses attract bears, elk, mule deer, mountain lions, badgers, grouse, wolves, whitetail deer, and migratory songbirds. Long ago Tom fenced miles of riparian corridor, which has resulted in the restoration of woodlands and an increase in migrating birds.

The main house was, in some years, used to house and feed ranch crews while the owners moved into the bunkhouse. These arrangements changed over time as needs dictated. Interiors of the house were dictated by need, too. The three little doors under the staircase are the result of a modification in the 1950s, and the cabinets in the kitchen were added by a previous owner. The floors of the draft horse stalls were milled from cottonwood logs, since cottonwood resists deterioration from the continuous wear and tear and the moisture of stabled horses. All the stone used by the masons was gathered on the ranch; the latest pieces of mossy stone were selected individually, while earlier masonry employed the miscellaneous rock, mostly sandstone, that was gathered while clearing fields and meadows. Interior doors were recently added, and a small alcove on the south side of the living room was introduced to add more light than was supplied by

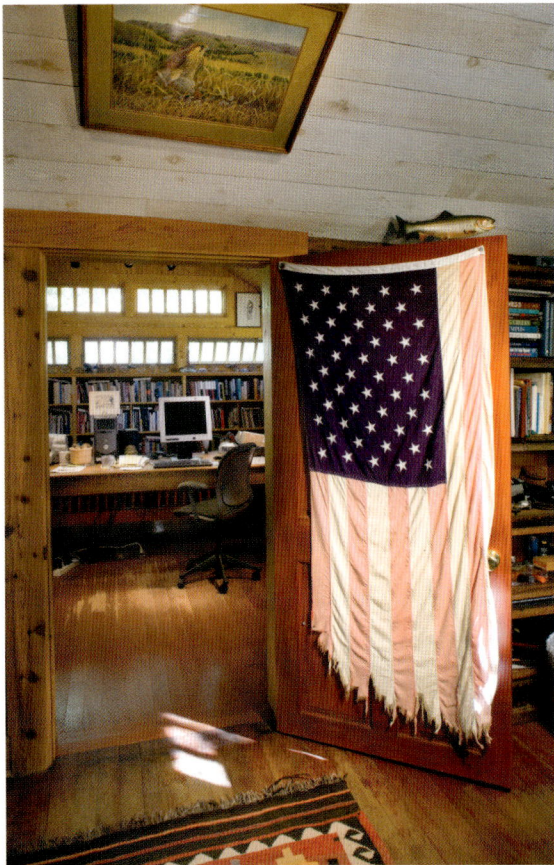

ABOVE: The entrance to the writer's refuge.

RIGHT: A personal library.

ABOVE: A guest room on the main level. There is a small storage space above the door.

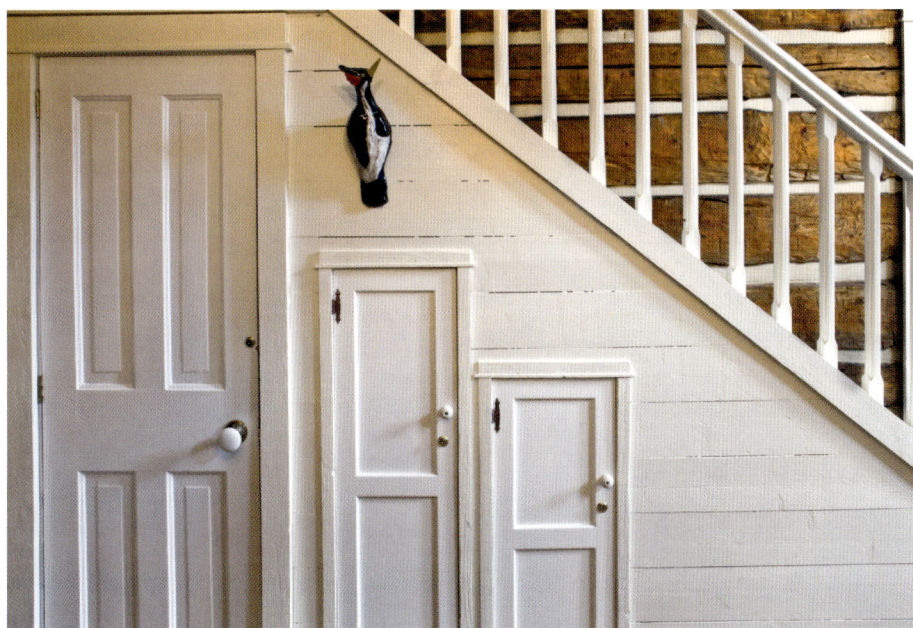

LEFT: A 1950s modification to the storage under the staircase.

Shining Mountain Ranch, *Montana*

A native of the West from the Utah and Idaho region, the owner of the Shining Mountain Ranch has created a secluded family retreat that embraces his family heritage of moving cattle and ranching. The goal was to build a ranch that might have existed in the late-nineteenth century, with architectural references to national park lodge architecture. The mountains of west-central Montana are rich in history. The

Bitterroot Mountains caused the greatest strife for the Lewis and Clark expedition, and campsites where Lewis and Clark struggled for survival are part of this landscape. Big Hole National Battlefield, a memorial to the people who fought and died in a five-month conflict that came to be called the Nez Perce War of 1877, is just ten miles west of Wisdom, Montana. Ancient Indian pictographs and petroglyphs are a tribute to the tribes that were forced from this land.

This timeless location was prime for the siting of the ranch. The 4,500-acre property would include a new owner's residence, a new working ranch cen-

LEFT: The front walk and main entrance to the ranch house.

ter, the lodge, and a number of guest cabins. When purchased, the ranch included a scattering of older ranch structures: barns, stables, horse corrals, and ranch-hand housing. Together, the owner and his architect, Doug S. Ewing of Ewing Architects, Inc., from Pasadena, California, designed a new master plan that satisfied the owner's desire to create a cohesive working cattle ranch alongside a place to introduce friends, visitors, and business associates to the unique quietude of the Bitterroots. They sited the new, extensive lodge building in a pine grove a quarter mile from the center of the ranch acreage. It has views through the pines to the south, down through a vast meadow hugged on all sides by the range.

ABOVE: Afternoon light filters through the trees.

RIGHT: A stone-and-log rear terrace off the great room. Steps lead to the trails.

Every day cattle and elk can be seen grazing among wildflowers in the meadow.

The main floor of the lodge, the gathering place on the ranch, has a very simple plan consisting of eight rooms: a mud room entry in the stone tower, an entry foyer with a warming fire, a great room with a dining area and a large fireplace at one end, and a lounge and reading area at the opposite end. A long, western-style bar, featuring custom-made iron-and-

leather bar seating, is fitted into an alcove on one side of the great room under the second-level balcony. There is a commercial kitchen—a necessity for the large gatherings that often take place at the lodge— and a pine-poled beam-and-stone study with a gorgeous inglenook fireplace that allows one to sit close to the fire on the precision-crafted stone benches. All the rooms open through several sets of full-height, glass-paned, French doors onto the south-

facing veranda and pastures beyond. Saddled horses are sometimes standing ready, a few steps away, in the shade of a circle of pine trees.

The second floor of the lodge has a sleeping room and dressing room. The bedroom was added in case the chef gets caught in a late-night snowstorm. The owner also stayed there during construction of the main house. There is an attractive sitting room along the balcony, with views into the great room

below and also out to the southern meadows. The lower floor is completely designed in structural stone, which has a slight resemblance to a castle wall. A theater for films and plays at the center of this level provides a getaway from the wild outdoors.

The inspiration for the lodge building is found in traditional Japanese architecture; in the tower, for example, the building becomes lighter and more tapered. Each plane is set back as it becomes higher.

OPPOSITE: The ranch entry at dusk.

UPPER RIGHT: An old cabin was moved to the site and restored as the "School Marm" guesthouse.

LOWER RIGHT: The great porch with reflections from the inside of the great room.

Larger-scale, heavier materials are found at the base of the building, and smaller-scale materials are at the top. The architect designed tapered walls with very large stones at each base receding to smaller stones at the top. Thus the building has a very powerful-looking base, grounding it to the natural landscape.

The post-and-beam log structure was built with natural logs of Engelmann spruce and lodge-pole pine. The building has double hips at the roofs, which are extremely rare, if found at all, in other structures made of log. The roof is unique in that it was designed to blend into the pine grove with stepped layers, or tiers. It steps up the ridge in three or four tiers, using smaller sizes of slate as it moves upward, creating a forced perspective. Rustic, heavy slate descends in size from 12″ x 3/4″ to 6″ x 3/8″ at the ridge, where it disappears into the tree line. Local Montana moss rock was used to form the six- and seven-foot tapered bases of the exterior walls. Popcorn burl logs were used on the interior hand railings and in the bar facing. The concept of "pattern graphics" was taught to the architect by an old Japanese gardener. The use of this concept creates a continuity of the design motif, as when elements such as the popcorn burl repeat in various manners and locations. Pattern graphics are best used in subtle and careful placement, with caution not to use more than two individual motifs.

LEFT: The decidedly western bar has custom stools
of iron and leather.

BELOW: A carved sideboard in the staircase alcove.

OPPOSITE: The living room area faces the fireplace at
the west end of the great room.

The Shining Mountain Ranch has many person-
alities. The architect wanted the heavy, fortresslike
stone on the north side to shed winter snow buildup,
sustain ferocious weather and winds, and use that
protection against the wilderness to emphasize the
warmth and security within. Another facet of the
design is his treatment of the south side of the lodge,
where full-height glass windows extend onto protected
verandas for solar gain, natural light, and views of
the southern landscape.

LEFT: The great room dining area and balcony toward the east of the room.

ABOVE: A detail of the stair landing to second floor.

OPPOSITE UPPER LEFT: The mud room at the entry.

OPPOSITE LOWER LEFT: The gallery corridor on the lower level.

OPPOSITE RIGHT: A view into the study.

ABOVE: A second-level reading and conversation room off the balcony.

ABOVE RIGHT: The screening room lounge.

RIGHT: The screening room is set up for a feature.

LEFT: The living and dining areas of the School Marm cabin.

BELOW: A bedroom with fireplace in the School Marm cabin.

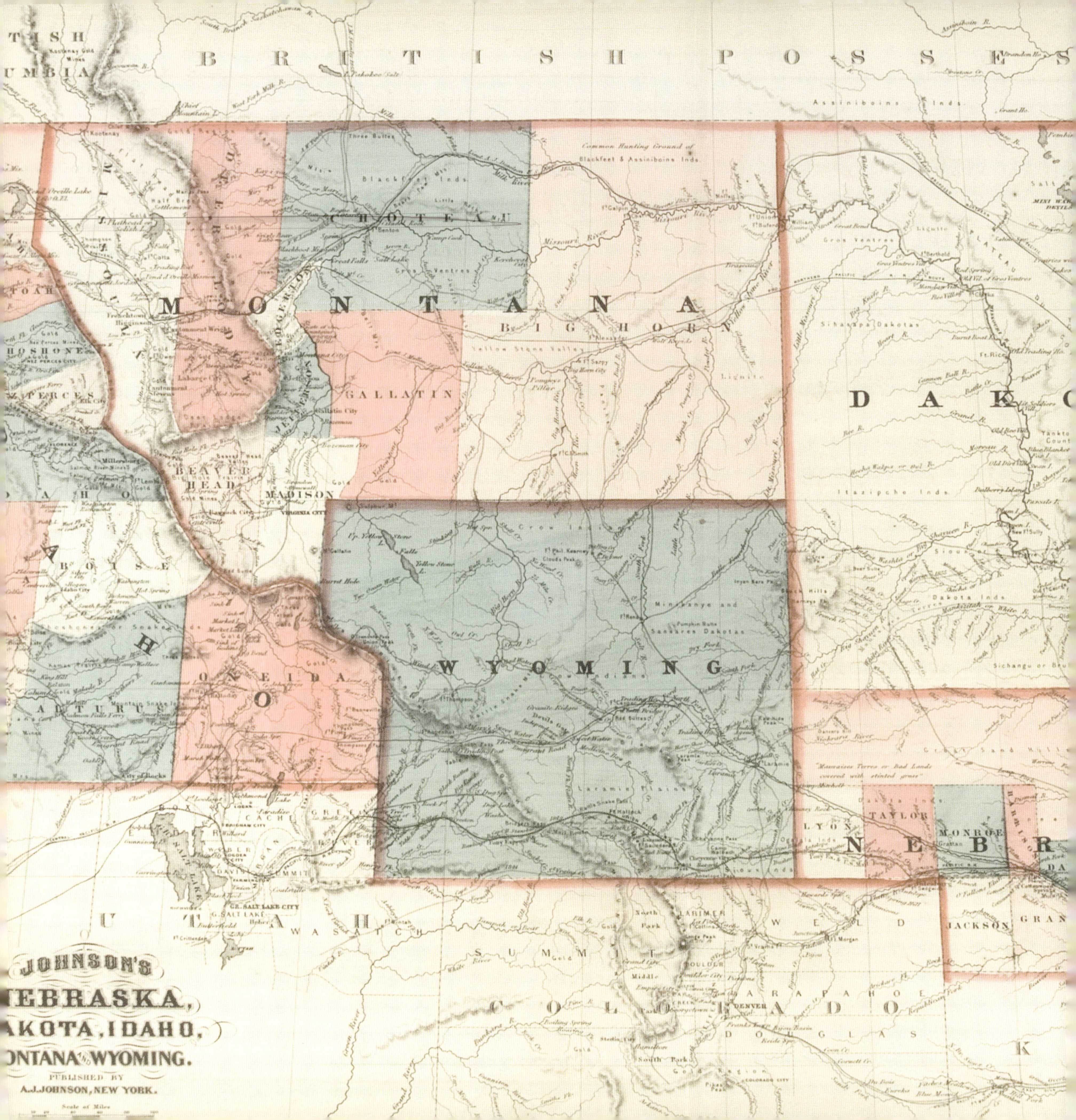

BRITISH POSSES

BRITISH COLUMBIA

MONTANA

CHOTEAU

BIG HORN

GALLATIN

BEAVER HEAD

MADISON

IDAHO

BOISE

DAKO

DAKOTA

WYOMING

ONEIDA

UTAH

WASATCH

NEBR

TAYLOR

LYON

MONROE

JACKSON

GRAN

WELD

COLORADO

DENVER

ARAPAHOE

DOUGLAS

JOHNSON'S
NEBRASKA,
DAKOTA, IDAHO,
MONTANA & WYOMING.
PUBLISHED BY
A.J. JOHNSON, NEW YORK.
Scale of Miles

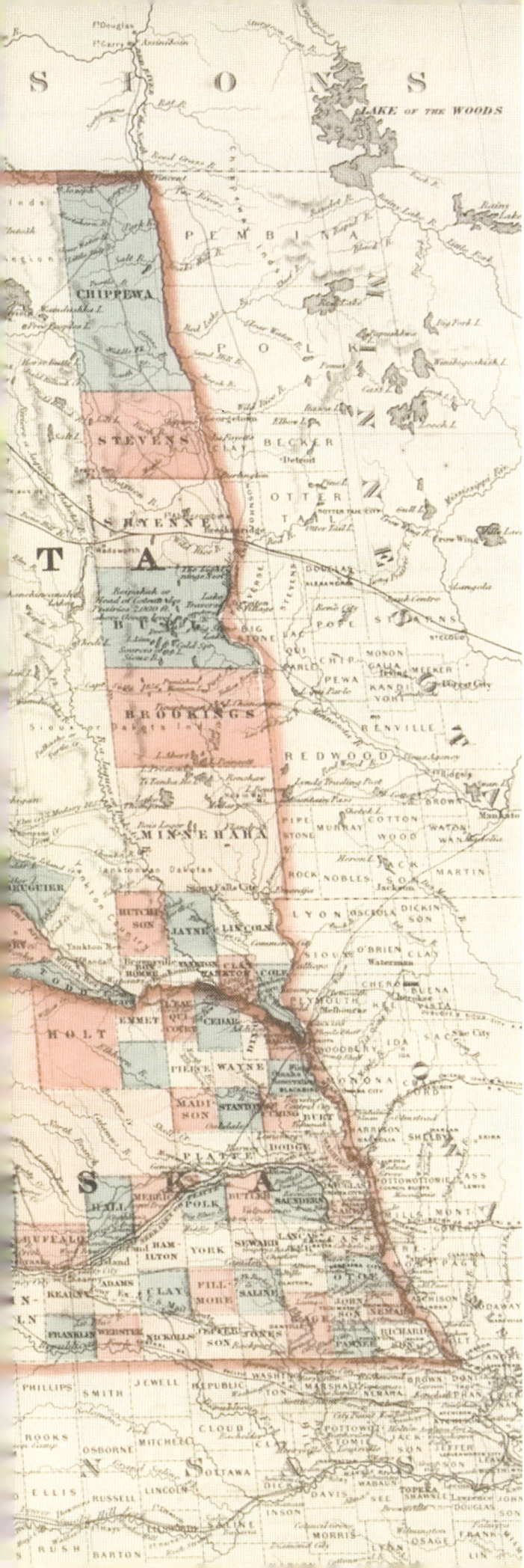

Part III: *The Great Plains*

"There was nothing unusual in the structures of the ranch…the typical layout…a main building, a cowboy's bunk house, a barn with open shed attached, a hitching bar, two or more corrals…a windmill and watering troughs." (Philip Ashton Rollins, The Cowboy, An Unconventional History of Civilization on the Old-Time Cattle Range, *1936). The end of a long cattle drive, of sleeping under horses and tarps in snow, rain, or sun, meant the dream of a fine log house had become an ideal.*

Teton Valley Ranch, *Wyoming*

This Teton Valley ranch in northwest Wyoming feeds off the meandering, oxbow loop of the Buffalo River. Eye-catching trumpeter swans and easily recognizable sandhill cranes have mapped the higher elevation wetlands for seasonal visits along with mallards and the gadwall, Cinnamon Teal, Northern Pintail, and Green-winged Teal species of duck. All sojourn here, one of the most productive waterfowl-breeding habitats on the continent.

Wyoming has thousands of miles of mapped migration corridors for seven big-game species. Elk, bighorn sheep, mountain goats, and moose are among those migrating at higher elevations. The elk corridor from Yellowstone and Teton National Park is further protected and has become a safe haven by a conservation easement placed on the private ranch lands by its owner. Hordes of moose may be seen standing in the oxbow of the freezing river scavenging for willows at the water's edge as part of the winter passage to Jackson. Thousands of elk move across the ranch each year to fresher grounds after a brief stay en route to their refuge in Jackson. Spring returns the elk to Yellowstone and the Teton wilderness on a journey of fifty to one hundred miles.

RIGHT: The Corral Creek Ranch sits below the alpenglow-covered Grand Tetons.

FOLLOWING PAGES: The marshes below the ranch are part of the winter range for elk.

LEFT: The rear porch has unequaled views of the western landscape. French doors lead from the living room to the porch. The boulder staircase leads to the paths below.

BELOW LEFT: Under a covered porch is the front door entry. A bronze plaque of a Native American buffalo hunt, which was designed by Charles Rumsey and originally forged for the Manhattan Bridge in New York City, is inlaid in the timbered door.

BELOW RIGHT: A staircase of boulder and stone overlooks marshes to the mountain range.

OPPOSITE: The uncovered back patio terrace features bark-on cedar posts. The railings are horizontal lodge pole woven in a zigzag pattern. Beyond are the windows of the radial reading room off the master bedroom.

The owners searched for a working ranch that had good water and a history of successful cattle ranching. This working ranch, owned by the Rockefeller family until 1955, is one of the last private properties that is surrounded by public parkland. The ranch came with a lodge that could accommodate six small guest suites upstairs and master quarters down-

ABOVE: A detail of the fly-fishing table. Montana artist David Laitinen wound old fishing reels into small wormwood pine poles and burl.

BELOW: A radial reading room off the master bedroom. A barn door slides closed for privacy.

RIGHT: The main entry and living room to the right, with dark-hewn timbered walls, twenty-foot Harlowton moss rock fireplace, and fallow deer chandelier. Above the mantel is *Blackfeet Camp at Crescent Moon* by Michael Coleman.

stairs. On the ranch, longhorn roping cattle are raised, along with a colorful posse of quarter horses. The owners were eager to begin the architectural process for their home and asked their friend, Diana Beattie, for help, after visiting the Double D Homestead, Diana's Montana ranch. Diana became the project manager on an invigorating and intricate project.

The design plan mandated that this historic property have an equally historic treatment. Some of the materials specified were one-hundred-year-old hewn timbers, which carpenters spent hours dovetailing in the fashion of old Wyoming construction. Cedar bark-on posts were used as the front entry and in the back, where the porch and terraces merge into the landscape, the bark creating a deep, three-dimensional surface that blurs delineations. The moss-covered Harlowton rock from Montana was chosen piece by piece for specific indoor and outdoor fireplaces, chimneys, and foundations. The materials

make the house appear as an original homestead, though it was added to the ranch later than the earlier buildings.

Towering above the homestead is the full power of the Teton Mountain Range. The building sits at the base of the foothills, below grazing fields and behind traditional jack fences, which are "gentle against the cows and horses," says Beattie. The central section contains the long-hewn-wood foyer, formal living room, and family room. The two-story section houses a guest suite in the lower front, and on the second floor is the children's wing with three bedrooms, baths, and a central lounge.

The one-hundred-year-old timber forms a wall separating the foyer from the living room. There is an oil of Lewis and Clark standing over the oxbow of the Missouri River, and kilim rugs soften the circular swan fir flooring. The living room repeats the dark hewn timbers in the walls, embellished by

the Harlowton moss-rock fireplace that rises twenty feet into a raftered ceiling. Two red chenille sofas provide a shock of color, but nothing can rival the images of the Grand Tetons seen through the three sets of French doors and windows. The dining room is set into a paned glass box of the large, open family room overlooking the marshlands, where the Buffalo River forms concentric circles of waterways below the mountains. Diana used subtle colors inside to emphasize the spectacular natural variations in color outside. Two chandeliers, one over the dining table, the other in the family room, were designed to feature the brands of the neighboring ranches, aged conchos, and petite sheep-hide shades. The family room is long, spanning thirty-four feet, and opens into a large, eat-in kitchen. The kitchen and bayed breakfast area open onto the patio, where there is an outdoor fireplace and barbecue under a pergola. While dining under the pergola or lounging on the patio, guests are always captivated by the winding waters, green grasses, and mountain patterns.

The master bedroom, surrounded by windows and endless views, needed additional privacy. A sliding barn door solved the need with a rustic flair. The suite of rooms contains a bedroom with a stone fireplace and stone wall, a radial sunlit reading room, his-and-her's baths, and dressing rooms. Three of the walls are stacked with hewn timbers, and the back wall was painted with several layers of glazing to achieve the warm rosy-peach color seen behind the bed and on the walls of the radial reading room. The bed is made of two Indian trellised doors, discovered by the owner's wife. The rounded stone turret studded with vertical windows was originally designed as an interior stairway leading to a lower level. The design was changed after seeing how much light was

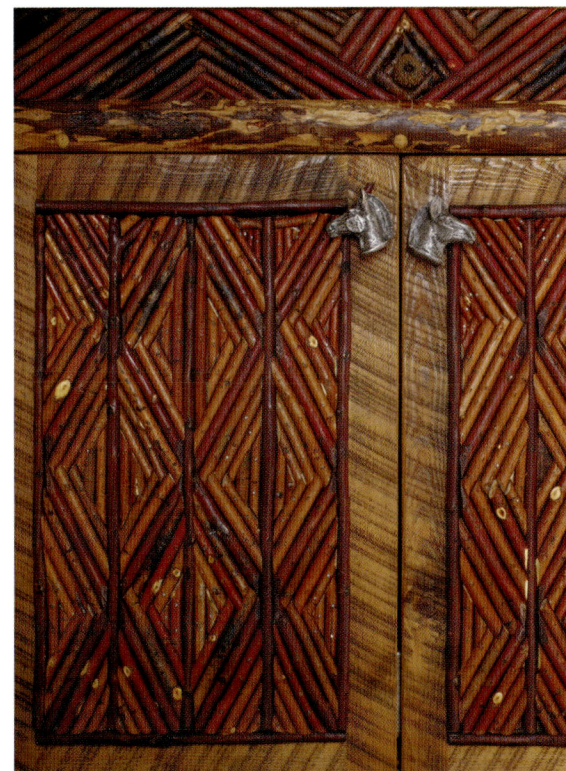

OPPOSITE: A girl's bedroom with the sunrise and sunset colors of Riverton Red Rock.

LEFT: A detail of the daughter's vanity made by David Laitinen.

ABOVE: The powder room is wallpapered with trail maps. Designer Diana Beattie scaled each map to include the exact location of the ranch.

delivered through the nearly floor-to-ceiling windows. Now it has become a wonderful space for morning coffee and nighttime reading.

The goal of the design was to allow the house to disappear into the landscape. The log structure is almost masked by the Douglas fir trees that step down the hillside. The golden colors of sheep fescue planted around the house blend with the natural and wild grasses of the riverbed landscape. Spring wildflowers and young aspens surround the one-hundred-year-old hewn-log structure.

ABOVE: Drawers and cupboards frame the way to the saloon doors that lead into the husband's dressing room and bath.

RIGHT: The master bedroom is surrounded by windows that led to the addition of the radial reading room for privacy. The view from this room is unsurpassed.

West Pass Ranch, *Wyoming*

At the foot of the Big Horn Mountains on the border between Wyoming and Montana is the West Pass Ranch, near Sheridan. In 1939 a plan was promoted by Sheridan city elders to form a new state from sections of northern Wyoming, southeast Montana, and western South Dakota. The new state would be named *Absaroka*, the Crow Indian name for those who inhabited much of south-central Montana. "This area was always considered the best country by the Indians," says the owner of West Pass Ranch, "which was why there were so many battles here." The best

known is the Battle of the Little Bighorn, which took place in 1876 only forty miles from the ranch.

Two distinct mountain ranges comprise the Absaroka-Beartooth Wilderness, and they are different in climate, elevation, plant communities, and wildlife. To the west lie the Absarokas, a landscape

LEFT: Sunrise at the West Pass Ranch in Wyoming.

BELOW: A selection of chairs surrounds an old timbered harvest table on the back porch.

of volcanic and metamorphic rocks, forested valleys, and rugged peaks. The high granite plateaus of the Beartooth Mountains dominate the eastern side of the wilderness. Hundreds of lakes lie among the rock and alpine tundra, and some provide fishing for cutthroat, rainbow, and brook trout. Fishing in the Beartooths is limited to the high mountain lakes, where the country is austerely beautiful and extremely fragile. The owner of the West Pass Ranch believes in the value of small ecosystems and the health and vitality of the plants and creatures that reside within them. She thinks that ranchers are stewards of those systems; that a good rancher is an environmentalist who is intimately connected with the land.

The owner's roots and family are largely from the East, and she wanted a house that would make a "hybrid" like her feel at home. She wanted a harmonious blend of western hewn-log cabins, using

OPPOSITE: The front entrance and side porch show the recycled timbers and flat-cut-stone exterior.

RIGHT: The ranch house's porches, balconies, and covered patio atop a rolling hill.

BELOW LEFT: Freshly cut hay in the fields, waiting to be baled.

restacked log buildings for the patina and character, and requested a two-story building and the occasional odd-shaped room, as these were features remembered with fondness from her grandparents' house. She also requested features from the High Victorian tradition found in New York City's Dakota apartment building: elongated doors and windows, thick plaster walls, beautiful wood moldings, and paned windows. The owner asked that the rooms be situated in such a way that the sun would follow her activities throughout the day. She hired Kipp Halvorsen, of Faure Halvorsen Architects in Bozeman, Montana, who creatively extended her vision in multiple ways.

The house was designed to be reminiscent of early childhood in the East, but without replicating an eastern-style house. The shapes and sizes of rooms are based on period homes of the early 1800s, which had in turn inspired the look and scale of the ranch house. This progression in layout was not very different from the way the West was settled. People from the East influenced the first homes of a "style" in the area, and their influences are found to dominate much of the true architecture of the Old West. Many wives would not leave their eastern or European houses until their homes were duplicated, room for room, in the West—a testament to many historical western architectural roots. The West Pass Ranch is the same in its initial conception, but the hybrid nature of the house is unique; the raw and refined Victorian combination resulted in a new "indigenous" style. The use of recycled oak, pine, and fir for flooring, old tin tiles on the porches, custom doors and windows, and interior sandstone walls adds a stalwart force to the Victorian lines. A simple interior color palette keeps the visual context quiet enough to emphasize the purity of raw architecture. The furniture is a mix of family antiques and art that the owner's parents collected when they lived in Europe, western pieces found at auctions or shops, and some contemporary pieces.

Spring calving and two spring brandings are part of the annual cycle of the operation. In summers the cattle are turned out to graze on wild grasses. In the fall calves are weaned and it is selling time, before the slower pace and shorter days of winter.

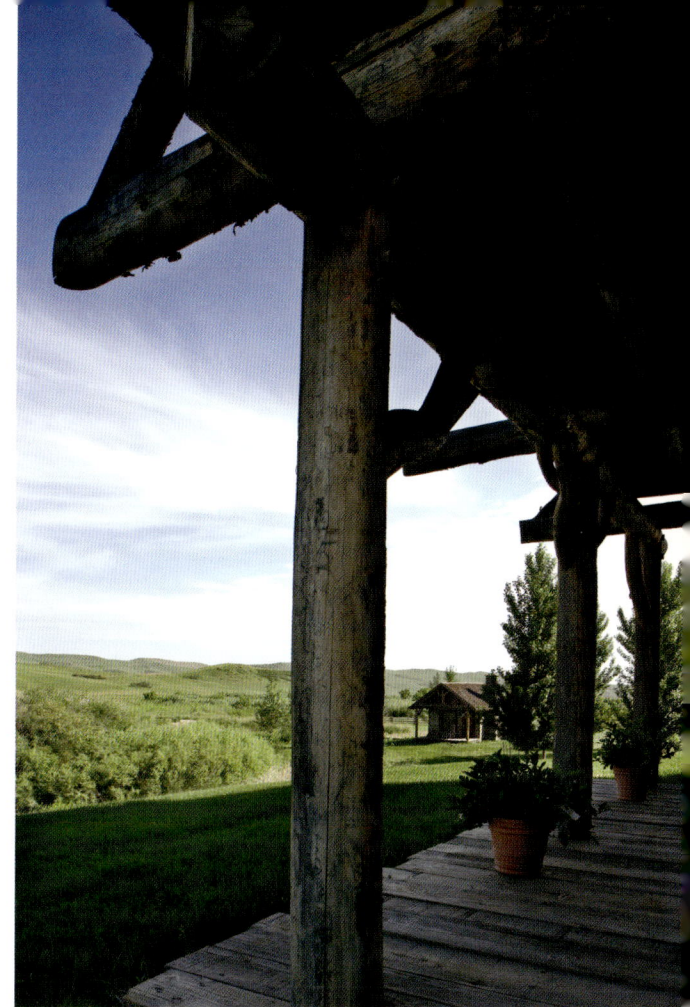

OPPOSITE: West Pass in the valley under the clouds.

UPPER RIGHT: A view of the guesthouse and the hills beyond.

LOWER RIGHT: The guest cabin and willow chairs on the porch.

LEFT: Heavily timbered rafters and walls form a two-story open room for living and dining areas. The kitchen is beyond the dining table.

ABOVE: The front door and gallery foyer step down into the main room.

OPPOSITE: The stone fireplace reaches twenty-five feet to the ridgeline of the roof. Upper-story windows admit natural light, and stairs lead to a small balcony.

OPPOSITE: The master bedroom and a view of the valley.

LEFT: Family heirloom and border collie imitate the art above.

BELOW: Quilts and saddles furnish a guest bedroom.

Diamond G Ranch, *Wyoming*

The owner of the Diamond G left his Manhattan office in 1988 to fulfill his ideal of living a traditional western life. He purchased a ranch located at the end of a lush valley surrounded by the Tetons, Gannett Peak, and Cloud Peak, all over thirteen thousand feet in elevation in the Rocky and Big Horn mountain ranges. The river and stream waters from all three mountains drain through the Dunoir Creek River and run through Diamond G land, twenty-three miles southeast of Yellowstone and Grand Teton national parks. It is the archetypal mountain wilderness, sublime with dizzying elevations, alpenglow, ranging beasts, and rushing waters. Even here a "traditional

western life, plain and simple" is difficult to find and alive with contradiction.

The owner's desire to have the ranching life means raising cattle, spending the day on horseback, and living with ranch values. Several years ago he and his ranch manager had trouble getting the cattle to stay on the mountain summer range. The fourth

BELOW: The original restored ranch house of the Diamond G Ranch.

RIGHT: The spread of the Diamond G buildings in the autumnal valley.

LEFT: The original ranch house was restored to its functional character by the owner.

ABOVE: The new barn designed by Jonathan Foote. The upstairs has a game room, conference room, and office; the lower floor houses barn equipment.

time they took them up, about five or six miles from home, they got to the summer range, settled them down, sat with them for hours, and then rode home. On the way home it hailed hard and they had to dismount and take shelter under their horses. When the hail stopped, they heard a thunderous roar and watched the entire herd charge past them, crashing through gates, and head home. The two men just sat

on the ground, soaking wet, and laughed for half an hour. Western people, he says, expect things to go wrong and take it in stride. The western maxim "If you don't get bucked off today, you will be tomorrow," is one to remember.

The owner bought the ranch from the Walt Disney family, who had purchased it in 1968 as their refuge. It had been an operating cattle ranch since before 1920. When sold in 1988 to the current owner, the operation began running eight hundred cow and calf pairs until last year, when the program was changed to yearlings. A large new barn was built on the property, designed by notable ranch architect Jonathan L. Foote. In 1973 Foote sold his own farm in Connecticut and headed west to become a cowboy. He found architectural inspiration in the materials and craftsmanship of the old dude ranches. His work is recognizable by an unmatched purity of line from square-cut timbers and by its scale. It is neo-postmodernist, slightly industrial, and essentially spiritual in form. The materials are from the old catalogs; exterior wood planks are stained to reflect age. The barn designed on the Diamond G Ranch has an office and a large meeting room in the upstairs. Downstairs there is a wood shop, a machine shop, and storage. Many old-timers who visit the ranch say, "well, it looks like a barn, but there are too many windows." The owner initially had a conference room upstairs, where there is a large, rectangular window at either end of the barn from which the historic ranch house can be seen directly across the yard. A string of smaller windows runs along each side of the barn at the base of a "popped-up" roofline. The room inside has been converted to a post-meeting poolroom.

The spread in the center of this multicolored valley has the Foote barn, five or six low ranch buildings, the wranglers' cabins, the ranch manager's house, and the owner's new house about a mile from the historic ranch house. The historic house has been restored to its original style by the owner. At New York's Secondhand Rose he purchased period linoleum flooring for the glass-enclosed front porch. Six sets of triple-paned windows, each containing thirty-six small windows, surround the porch, which is filled with sunshine and gladiolus. A buffalo trophy is a reminder of what once stood right outside the windows. Lovely vertical paned windows open into the kitchen, which, like the porch, is clad in white bead board. French doors open from the kitchen to the living room. A de Angeles sofa appears aboriginal in its antique army blanket upholstery on a standout Navajo rug. Opposite are two comfortable, red leather and wood Molesworth chairs. Variable width painted wood flooring meets wood-paneled walls and deep-set wood-framed windows in the living room. Lightbulbs without shades drop from the ceiling for utility. The back door has a mudroom with chairs for removing boots and wood pegs for hanging chaps, saddlebags, canteens, hats, and jackets.

OPPOSITE: The front porch with vintage linoleum flooring from New York's Secondhand Rose. Wicker and branch furniture fills the room.

RIGHT: Buffalo and geraniums in the sun porch.

BELOW: A back-door mudroom for the cowboys.

The Wyoming Nature Conservancy has determined that the Diamond G Ranch is the most biologically diverse and important piece of land in private hands in the state of Wyoming. Grizzly bears, wolves, lions, and badgers roam the range. Elk, deer, and antelope are prey, as are cattle, horses, and dogs. Beavers and otters engineer the rivers.

OPPOSITE: The living room is furnished with red leather and wood Molesworth chairs and Navajo rugs. The kitchen is in the room through the French doors.

RIGHT: The poolroom in the upstairs section of the barn.

BELOW LEFT: The owner's office on the second floor of the barn. The house can be seen through the window behind the desk.

BELOW RIGHT: A detail of the twig cabinet in the poolroom.

Bear Lodge and Cub Cabin, *Wyoming*

Very few people look for property from a hot-air balloon, but that was the only way to consider the route of the Gros Ventre and Snake rivers in Jackson Hole. The land was so dense with spruce and cottonwood trees that Dan and Gail Cook felt it was best viewed from above. It was part of the famous Hansen Ranch—Clifford Hansen was a rancher, former governor, and senator from Wyoming. The Cooks envisioned a full, traditional log lodge reminiscent of 1930s hunting lodges. They turned to longtime friend, Chicago architect James L. Nagle, to design their country retreat.

The architect's approach was to build a series of log pavilions, beginning with a two-bedroom guesthouse called Cub Cabin that would be some distance

LEFT: The buildings of Bear Lodge are built of logs and stone and covered with copper roofing.

BELOW: A herd of "Dan's elk" moving through the trees.

from Bear Lodge. The framing, logs, windows, and details of the guesthouse, which provided quarters for the owners while the lodge was under construction, were used to test the design approach for other structures. Eventually, five lodge pavilions were linked together in an informal way, following the contours of the land and directing the views toward the Teton Mountains and the rivers. The central great room of the lodge has granite fireplaces at either end of the large, two-story space, with a balcony of burl wood railings all around. The flanking pavilions, which are connected by bridges, contain a family room with childrens' bedrooms above on one end, and the master suite with an office and sitting room at the opposite end. The other pavilions include a care-taker's room, garages, and a sport gear room. All buildings were built with logs from standing dead trees found on the property; the bark was hand-stripped on site. Low-pitched copper roofs that cap the hunting lodge will weather nicely on the remote site and fade into the evergreen branches.

The interiors have log walls and antique chestnut floors, with moss-covered rock, fifty-million-year-old fossil stone, handmade tiles, and dozens of antique doors bought by the Cooks in Spain. Gail had required a native ruggedness and commissioned large, forged-iron chandeliers and wall sconces of old ranch branding irons for the great room. She also selected all the burled logs used for the columns, balconies, and built-in shelves and cabinets.

ABOVE: One of the large antique wood-and-iron double doors purchased by the owners in Spain.

RIGHT: A collection of copper kettles and a bear under the knarly wood railing of the staircase.

OPPOSITE: The great room features a quintessential collection of original Molesworth pieces. The overhead chandeliers are made of branding irons.

To furnish the lodge the owners assembled the most inclusive collection of Thomas Molesworth furniture and accessories in the world. They appreciate the pieces for being American and western. At first they weren't sure that they would be able to find enough Molesworth furniture to fill Bear Lodge and Cub Cabin, but Terry Winchell of Fighting Bear Antiques in Jackson Hole provided his expertise to locate pieces, including seventy items that were commissioned in the 1930s for a lake lodge in the east.

There are amazing Molesworth fireplace screens, each with a scene that runs along the bottom, such as cattle and a covered wagon. The upper parts of the screens show delicate lines of iron in the shapes of clouds or birds. There are leather-strap chairs, small and large leather-topped tables, and even magazine racks. Molesworth created coffee tables, end tables, and lamp tables with sheepskin shades, carved stems, and little twig-trimmed skirts for an ashtray or drink. There are leather-topped banquet tables that seat

ABOVE LEFT: All of the draperies in the house were finished in beadwork done by the owner's wife, Gail. She spent one hour on each inch of beading, completing 5,400 inches of beadwork.

ABOVE RIGHT: An antler mirror and mica-and-copper lamp on the table.

OPPOSITE: The foyer features a large mosaic of a Native American in headdress.

LEFT: A stone stairwell, knarly railing, and wood-topped stone steps curve around a Swiss carved-bear candleholder.

ABOVE: A splendid Thomas Molesworth fireplace screen.

BELOW: A painting of a steer wrestler next to a wall of spurs and bridles.

twenty people, as well as chairs and sofas. Other westernalia at Bear Lodge includes Edward S. Curtis photographs, Navajo weavings, and Native American beadwork, baskets, and pottery. Swiss carved-bear furniture from the 1880s is joined by cowboy paraphernalia from Argentina, sculptures, and select paintings that blend splendidly with the antique furnishings. Gail created beaded work as edge trim on all the leather draperies in the lodge.

Willows, grasses, and wildflowers cover the landscape; this variety of plant life attracts moose, elk, and deer. The confluence of the two rivers and three spring-fed creeks completes a natural migration route for elk to cross the property in the fall

on their way to the Elk Wildlife Refuge, where they spend the winter before returning in the spring. Canada geese migrate across the property, and American eagles nest high in the trees. Hummingbirds can be heard "clicking" in the spruce trees, while woodpeckers, trumpeter swans, and cranes fill the air with abstract orchestrations. Continuous stream improvement is essential to ensure the best habitat for the trout. The owners have redone the trout streams twice, and like on every western property, their work is never done.

ABOVE: This bedroom is furnished with Molesworth furniture and Navajo rugs.

ABOVE RIGHT: The Thomas Molesworth collection of lamps and chests with figurative carvings and woven upholstery.

RIGHT: A curved Molesworth couch, blue leather and wood table, and matching chairs.

OPPOSITE: A Spanish *vega*-style ceiling and vertical pole wall offset the collection of Edward S. Curtis Native American photographs.

Colorado Ranch, *Colorado*

This magnificent ranch was first homesteaded in the late 1880s. When the present ranchers purchased it they became only the third owners. Virtually surrounded by National Forest land, the ranch is covered with pine trees and trout streams. The property, though spectacular, was in need of a bit of care. Stream restoration has been an ongoing project. The ranch resurrection focused on the barn and arena and also included an outdoor arena with a viewing space, a ranch manager's house, and an outdoor barbecue.

The main building's primary purpose is an indoor arena for rodeo. The architectural challenge was to nestle a very large building into the landscape while maintaining a scale appropriate to the existing ranch buildings on the property. The first idea was to place smaller-scale elements on the corners of the building as a signature of the overall structure. For instance, the entrance at the entertainment area is designed to be a "hay barn," which brings the scale down to a very human level. The guesthouse serves a similar architectural function. The second idea was to have the sloping topography of the mountain valley reflected by the forms of the building. Certain lines and windows slope imperceptibly, with the desired result of a manmade building that closely resembles the natural topographic stature of the land that surrounds it.

The arena, with its very large spans, is actually a premanufactured structure. All of the overhanging eaves are reclaimed structural timber frames, which were left exposed. The exterior materials are the same ones that have been used in the area for over a century: raw steel, wood siding, and a local Colorado Red Rose sandstone mixed with a brown buff sandstone—much of which came from the ranch. The

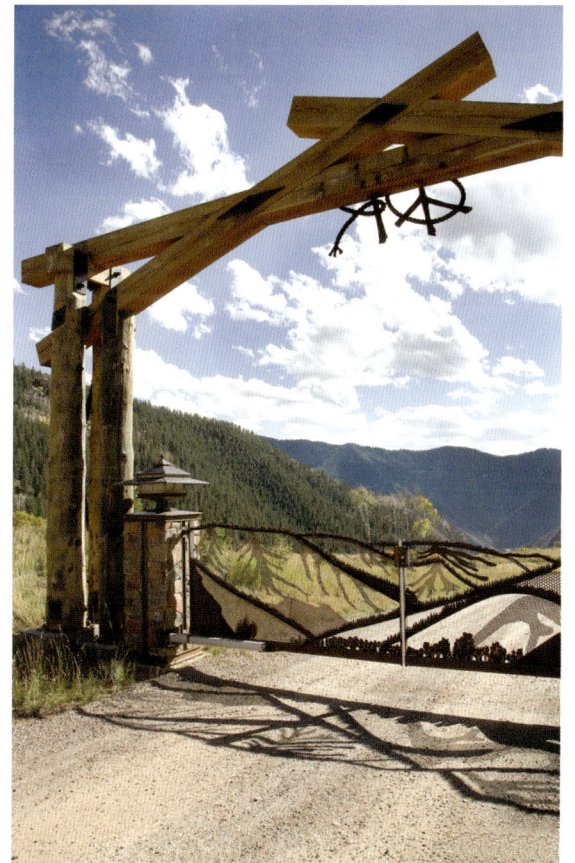

LEFT: The arena building, residential quarters, and barbecue building in the grassy valley.

roof is rusted steel in two configurations: corrugated and flat, overscaled sheets laid up like enormous shingles. The materials used on the interiors reflect the same spirit as those outside: simple, stripped down, and straightforward. Flooring is reclaimed, with hatched and saw indentations for character. Interior wood paneling is indigenous pine, and accents are unobtrusive steel or galvanized aluminum.

The participants in the rodeo activities are local ranchers or guests of the ranch, and the events are tailored to their interests. The ranch manager's daughter, for instance, is competing in barrel racing, a very popular event high on the list of activities. The arena building also houses a six-stall barn, covered hay storage, a tack room, and the ranch manager's office. The northeastern corner, adjacent to the outdoor area, is a second-story entertainment area and observation gallery that includes a full

PREVIOUS PAGES: A road to corrals, the stable, and the barn for the arena building.

ABOVE: An outdoor fireplace and patio attached to the residential quarters at the corner of the arena building.

RIGHT: The living room and fireplace of the residential quarters at the arena.

horseman's bar. The northwestern corner overlooks the stream, the ponds, and the ranch beyond. A cozy two-bedroom guesthouse is attached to the arena and has become the owners' favorite place to stay when they are on the ranch. The outdoor barbecue is a small building a few steps from the owner's quarters, overlooking the outdoor arena.

PEACE
HORSES AND
Basalt, C
CAMPFIRE
STORIES
TOLD HERE!

PROPRIETORS: MO

LEFT: The arena lounge area furnished with a Thomas Molesworth sofa and chairs. A small dining table, long bar, and viewing gallery run along the show floor.

ABOVE TOP: The interior stalls in the arena building.

ABOVE BOTTOM: The viewing gallery at the end of the show floor.

Lucky L Ranch, *Colorado*

At the lofty elevation of 9,600 feet, the Lucky L Ranch is steeped in the lore of the Old West and lively with the architecture of early ranch buildings. Set amid a grove of tall and wispy aspen beside a grassy, wildflower-strewn meadow, the house has a 180-degree view of the Dolores Mountain Range, the 14,246-foot peak of Mt. Wilson, Lone Cone, and Flat Top Peaks in southwestern Colorado near Telluride. The property was once a part of a much larger ranch owned by a local family that ran cattle and sheep for more than four generations. They are now friends of Tom and Ellen Likovich, whose new house is the expression of their respect for their land and the desire to minimize visual intrusion upon it. The site is always the starting point of a design. It may start as far away as twenty miles, but it is the beginning of the visual story that the house will tell; the introduction to the mountains and the aspens that will be framed by the design of the buildings.

The approach to the ranch leads to the barn, then through the rustic porte cochère to the tree-lined interior courtyard. The ranch design originated in the concept of breaking down and pulling apart large spaces to create individual rooms and cabins, and of using old materials in a modern way. The result is a grouping of log cabins that are tied to each other through long, wood-clad corridors. Each corridor interior has rustic planking, wood floors and ceilings; the side facing the landscape is set with large, framed windows that look upon outdoor decks, porches, breezeways between cabins, and the surrounding landscape. This layout allows a greater sense of harmony between the home and

LEFT: The road gate through the aspens to the ranch.

RIGHT: The connected cabins of the ranch step down from the hill, beginning on the right.

OPPOSITE: The road approaching the barn, which acts as a threshold to the house.

LEFT: Connected decks around the courtyard are visible from the interior corridor.

BELOW TOP: The identifiable Jonathan L. Foote trimmed-beam barn design.

BELOW BOTTOM: Signature JLF treatment of posts, beams, and angles on the barn interior.

FOLLOWING PAGES: A full moon after the snow illuminates the string of connected cabins.

the surrounding nature: the views were framed to bring the feel of the outside to the inside of the house. The great room and kitchen wing has glass end walls that allow one to see through the building, again blurring the edges of the interior and the landscape.

The cabins are situated at differing elevations and orientations that contribute to the feeling of a compound and create the human scale necessary in a large building complex. The connecting corridors pass through several cabins as they step down in elevation from the main entry and mudroom to a master suite with an office, a bunkhouse-style bedroom area, and the great room. The corridors are used as galleries, and a charming stair with branch railing off the corridor leads to an upstairs bedroom.

Each cabin is made of logs that show a century of hatchet and ax marks. The reclaimed materials, ancient stone, and galvanized metal roof materials give the architecture an impression of permanence, almost a historical quality, as if the house were not new but possibly a homestead ranch built at the turn of the century, with necessary buildings being added and restored over time.

The Likoviches wanted a ranch that would support a small herd of horses. They had vacationed with their daughters at dude ranches in Colorado and Idaho and decided they wanted a ranch of their own. They soon discovered that the ranches they found most appealing were designed by the firm of Jonathan L. Foote in Bozeman, Montana. Foote, too, is a rancher and horseman whose expertise lies in what he calls the "pure substance" of the old ranches. He is devoted to the reuse of old materials: timbers with bullet holes and rusty hooks. When he

RIGHT: The beauty of the wood is evident in this photograph of the end of the corridor descending toward the writing desk.

BELOW: The corridor that looks out over the courtyard and connects two cabins.

OPPOSITE: The liveliness of the living room design comes from the red paint used on the barn from which these planks were saved. The signature square-trimmed joists and posts, and wood for the dining table contrast with the flat-cut-stone walls.

first arrived in the West, old barns were being burned down, and he saw an opportunity to carry out his belief that the materials only needed to be respected and "reorganized."

One of the principles of Foote's architectural work is his belief in the materials' ability to dictate the scale of a room. In the great room, dining room, and kitchen, square-cut timbers create a vaulted ceiling supported by posts, beams, and open trusses. The wood ceiling planks are pieces of old red barn siding—large and long enough to define the size of the room. The red color is an extraordinary back-drop for the furniture and accents below, and works in concert with the reclaimed bleached beams and

OPPOSITE: The spacious living room with expansive windows and decks just outside.

ABOVE: The writing desk is at the bottom of the corridor that runs beside the courtyard. Above the stairs is the arched doorway of the next cabin.

FOLLOWING PAGE: The colors in the ceiling wood pick up tones from the rugs and complement the outer walls.

the light stacked-rock walls and fireplace. The architects designed the iron-and-wood chandelier and the long, thick-planked harvest table.

Cattle ranchers move their cattle to the Lucky L Ranch during the summers to benefit from the nutrient-rich grasses. The summer months are

filled with ranch chores—the corral needs to be cleaned, fences must be mended, fallen trees are chopped for firewood, and the pastures need tending. Less attention is required in winter, when everything is under three feet or more of snow, clear skies, and a bright moon.

GILLESPIE

Fredericksburg

Pittsburg

DWARDS

KERR

Sisterdale

San Mar

Puerto de la Bandera

COMAL

BANDERA

New Braunfels

GUAD

San Antonio

UVALDE

Hillsborough

Castroville

MEDINA

Dhanis

Leona Spr.

Fort Inge

New Town

FRIO

ATASCOSA

ZAVALA

Noble Mts.

Part IV: *Texas*

During the Texas revolt of 1836 the Mexicans were driven out of the land north of the Rio Grande. The Texans happily took over the abandoned Mexican ranches. The 1870s through the 1890s began an era when the historic ranches of Texas were established in their own style. The Matador Ranch built a sturdy chuck house and bunkhouses of local white limestone blocks and shingled roofs, as did the Cross B Ranch in 1877, the Two Buckle Ranch, and the JA Ranch. The materials were the same; differences in design varied only by which cultural reference was brought to the Texas plains.

Gallagher Ranch, *Texas*

The Gallagher Ranch and Headquarters might be found as the setting for a number of Cormac McCarthy Texas border novels. Peter Gallagher, a stalwart Irish civil engineer, came to America in 1829 to build the docks of New Orleans; later, in an era when the Spanish encouraged pirates to prey on French and English ships, he traveled to Galveston, then called "Galvez Town." Again, Gallagher found himself at the center of another barbaric world, this time to build the docks and wharves of Galveston along the low coastline. "It was while Gallagher was building the first Galveston wharves, that he became very solid with the Mexican government. Only a free agent, both in allegiance and determination, could have survived."[1]

In 1833 Gallagher was commissioned by Mexico's president Santa Anna to locate and plan a military supply depot and headquarters near San Antonio. He looked for an abundance of good water and fertile land. The land of his discovery was still a territory of Mexico when he topped a hill

LEFT: The Gallagher Ranch encloses the great lawn and patio trees.

BELOW: The old drive through the gate to the ranch arch.

[1] Dade Rayfield, "Legend of the Circle G," *True West Magazine*, November-December 1966: 30-61.

twenty-three miles from San Antonio and saw distant mountain peaks in front of the setting sun and the lush valley of the San Geronimo River below him. The deep canyons and rugged hills convinced him to claim ten thousand acres that would become the historic Gallagher Ranch in 1833, three years before the fall of the Alamo.

The first building to be constructed is believed to have been the fortress home. Two buildings erected by Gallagher and his force of 250 Mexican peasants formed the major part of the three wings of the sprawling ranch house. One of them, the fortress home, has two-foot-thick walls of solid native limestone that was quarried from the canyon running through Gallagher's ranch. Gallagher and his family were in hostile land inhabited by

OPPOSITE LEFT: The stone arch and courtyard. Stairs lead to the second-floor rooms.

OPPOSITE RIGHT: The side entry and curving stairs to upper rooms.

ABOVE: The afternoon angle of the Texas sun.

Comanches, Kickapoo, and Lipan Indians, where smoke signals rose into the blue sky during the daylight and council fires burned all around them at night. Port holes and rifle slits from which Gallagher fired during Indian attacks remain; it is a testament to the permanence of their work that the family survived repeated attacks and that the fortress home still stands.

The ranch was purchased by Vachel H. "Mac" McNutt for his family in 1927, when it had only six rooms and an attic. When Mr. McNutt died in a horseback riding accident, Mrs. McNutt (Mama Mac) decided to open a guest ranch, which she successfully operated for fifty years. Cowboy Will James was a frequent guest and wrote his *New York Times* best-selling novel *Lone Cowboy: My Life Story* while at the ranch in 1930. Mrs. McNutt, a natural hostess who vowed to keep their ancestral home maintained, was perpetually involved in adding onto, restoring, and caring for the ranch as it became more successful. Her maxim for architectural restoration was that she "wanted the place to look like it had pushed itself up from under the trees."

OPPOSITE: The dining alcove and bottom of the staircase.

ABOVE: An exotic table of shells, with anthropomorphic legs, against a floral settee, a painting, and the limestone walls.

RIGHT: A portrait of the *haciendado*'s young daughter in silk shirts and overcoat, supported by a farthingale.

Chris Hill, an architect himself and the ranch's current owner says, "the Gallagher Headquarters is an example of good architecture without an architect." He maintains that his job is to stay in keeping with the style that has so wonderfully evolved from the original work of Mr. Gallagher and Mrs. McNutt. The rambling South Texas–style ranch house is native stone, painted white, and bears a traditional tile roof. Mexican architectural influences include the design of the home on a grassy quadrangle, shaded by live

OPPOSITE: The large kitchen workspaces with elaborate table carvings and tile.

RIGHT: A reading table under the chandelier in the main living room.

oak trees that were ancient when Peter Gallagher first saw them.

Hill says, "the ranch was never fancy, nor ever will be. But we want to bring it alive again. This is something we think will happen slowly." As it had been out of use for a decade or more, it called for loving attention when Chris first found it and decided it was right for him. Despite the restoration needed, it was a beloved piece of history.

The house maintains its simplicity of stone walls, terra-cotta floors, and cypress-beamed ceilings. The massive living room with two fireplaces and the two wings containing nineteen bedrooms, each with its own bathroom and fireplace, are fitted with eighteenth- and nineteenth-century furnishings from Mexico and the southwestern United States, and antiques from Europe. Two adjoining bedrooms have been transformed into small sitting and dining rooms. The master bedroom next door features an eighteenth-century Italian tester bed draped with linen brocade.

Hill suggests that the theme tying all the rooms together is a religious one. "I like religious artwork. It's so fervent, so emotional. The most interesting is the most naive." The walls, mantels, and other surfaces are pedestals and backdrops for paintings, carved wooden crucifixes, and *santos*. In the quiet space of a sitting room, among the multitude of Mexican and Spanish Colonial art and artifacts, some of which still bear black smudges from the high flame of church candles, the cherished favorite piece

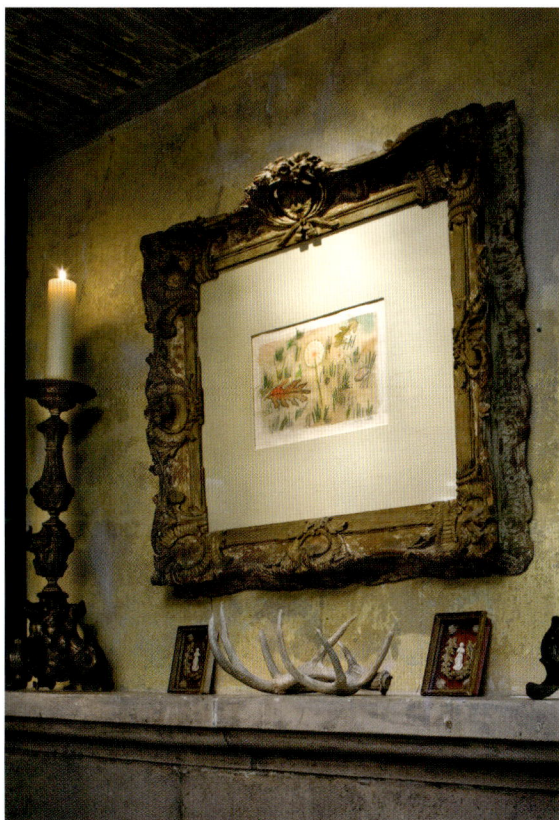

OPPOSITE: A bedroom with an antique four-poster canopy bed under the narrow, stripped bead-boards in the ceiling.

BELOW: A rare and delicate color sketch by Frida Kahlo.

RIGHT: A guest bedroom is furnished with a mix of antique fabrics and furniture.

of the Hill family hangs: a small, delicate, and rare drawing by Frida Kahlo.

Chris Hill claims the smooth limestone rock creek bed of the San Geronimo, which allows for fresh, clear water, is the most interesting feature of the ranch. Karst rock (also called popcorn rock) is found on the tops of the hills; it is the same rock that allows water storage and passage in the Edwards Aquifer—the sole water source for San Antonio that goes underground less than a quarter of a mile to the south of the ranch.

The Hill family has dedicated a 731-acre easement on the property to the Nature Conservancy of Texas. The lands around a nearby canyon are known to contain golden-cheeked warblers and other endangered songbirds. The land is populated by whitetail deer, wild turkey, and feral hogs. Red-shouldered hawks nest nearby, and the ranch is a habitat for the golden-cheeked warbler. Late summer is aglow with the migration of monarch butterflies on their way to western Mexico, and the caracara, known as the Mexican eagle, soars overhead. The Texas Hill country is the land of rolling hills, spring-fed canyons, heritage oak trees, and areas of dense cedar breaks. Native grasses such as side-oats gramma and introduced bluestem are staples for cattle, along with coastal hay produced on the Gallagher Ranch.

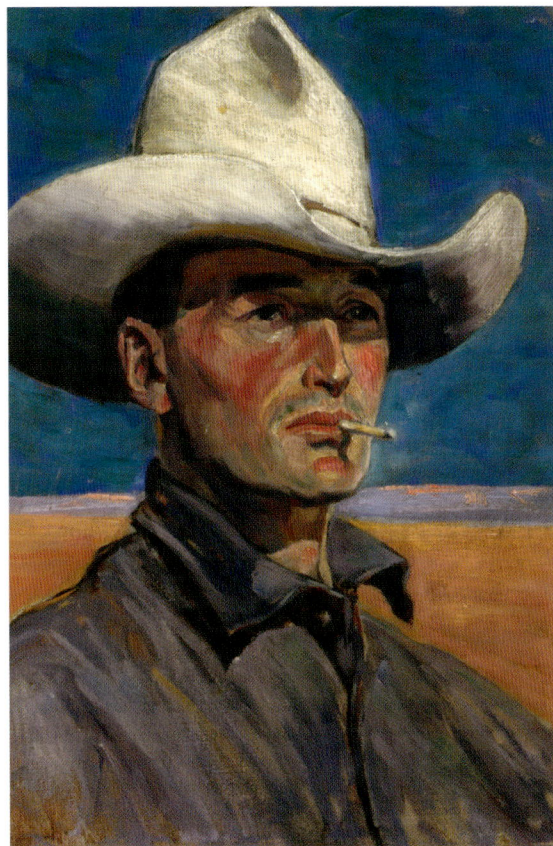

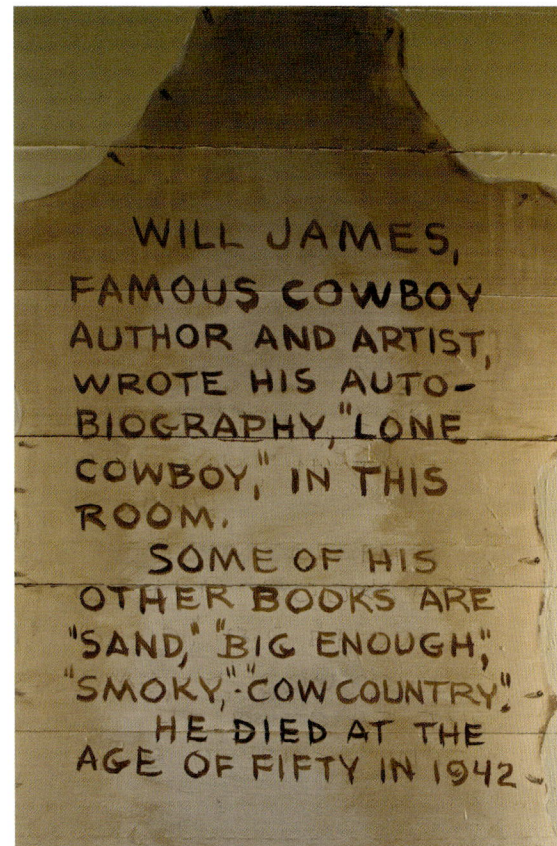

LEFT: A second-floor guest room once occupied by cowboy writer Will James.

ABOVE LEFT: Will James, *Self-Portrait*. Yellowstone Art Museum Permanent Collection, Gift of Virginia Snook. Reprinted with permission of the Will James Art Co., Billings, MT. 406.656-2851.

ABOVE RIGHT: A tribute to Will James on the guest-room wall.

Triple Creek Ranch, *Texas*

In Fredericksburg, Texas, there are very few historic houses, and those that remain are precious. "There is a tactile quality to ancient houses," says architect Donald B. McDonald. It is "classical proportion, craftsmanship, and detailing which will teach us more about previous cultures than any book could." This quiet vocabulary of building has passed among generations of carpenters, ironworkers, and stonemasons who built good houses, such as Triple Creek in 1855–65.

Triple Creek began as a cottage of stone (it was known as "the Cottage") that sat on a low rise in a

pasture near the confluence of three creeks. The realities of life in the Texas Indian Territory following the Civil War were far more arduous than the years leading up to it. Postwar additions to the cottage, meant to support domestic survival and endurance, included a large porch that covered

BELOW: The cottage facade and porch facing the great lawn.

RIGHT: The owner's cottage and three Sister Cottages on the right. "The Barn" great room and quarters face forward.

century electrification project was the last remnant of its evolution. Though deteriorated, the house was essentially a nineteenth-century time capsule.

A year was spent stabilizing the structure and doing research, ultimately establishing an improbable pedigree. The evidently well-proportioned facade was not accidental. Slowly, the influence of refined neoclassical high style in Germany at the time of construction became more apparent.

The millwork was well detailed, and the doors were expertly faux-grained, exhibiting the then-fashionable Biedermeier influence. The original cool green and pink color palette, and the beautifully executed rustification (the scoring of plaster to appear as cut stone), began to reveal that a sophisticated builder was then on the edge of the Texas frontier.

As the importance of the structure began to emerge, it became obvious that it deserved center stage in the development of the compound for this family. The Cottage was well sited to catch prevailing breezes, with a protected, yet sweeping view. The front porch looked out to the original approach from across the pasture. This view has not changed since the house was constructed, and the front of the house has remained intact, to be approached from the pasture on foot or horseback.

The balance of the compound is largely an architectural response to the stature of the Cottage, using the indigenous materials but detailed in a more restrained and twenty-first-century manner. Materials were selected to capture regional authenticity, and were generally obtained from within a fifty-mile radius of the compound. The region, settled late in Texas history by German natives, changed very little between 1850 and 1950, so the connection to history was close at hand and most surrounding structures

LEFT: An old cistern and original, functioning windmill.

the refined facade, and a hulking stone addition that engulfed the rear of the house.

Many years later a Houston couple visiting Fredericksburg discovered the Cottage, whose sole use over sixty years had been as a hay barn. Years of neglect and disrepair hadn't dimmed the allure of indigenous Texas stone and the exactitude of conformation, which escaped modification during remodeling or renovation efforts. The house was viewed as "a fine old antique," said McDonald, who specializes in architectural restoration projects of this kind. The structure had been taken out of domestic use for almost a century, and a crude, turn-of-the-

BELOW: Freshwater circulating in the pool.

RIGHT: A long loggia of rockers and chairs that runs along the cottages.

had changed little. The framing is longleaf pine salvaged from regional buildings. The roof is stainless steel, selected for its similar appearance to the original lead roofs of the region, which were laid over local cypress shingles with the ultimate effect of a soft skin, gently held by the shingles below.

Separate structures, called the "Sister Houses," were added to provide a large entertainment area and several bedrooms. The three houses are private, individual suites, built for the couple's three daughters.

LEFT: The living room and view to the dining room in the Cottage. The painting in the dining room is by Terri Kelly Moyers.

RIGHT: The patio fireplace and dining tables of the Barn gathering room.

Each house, of limestone and tidewater cypress, offers a sitting room, a lovely bedroom with French doors that open to the pasture and pool, and a dressing room. The Cottage, now restored, serves as the owners' residence. Narrow walkways run between the Sister Houses and the Cottage, and low walls run behind them, creating a narrow garden walkway shaded by a cedar "eyebrow" trellis.

The large communal building is called "the Barn" by the family. It is designed for living, dining, and entertaining in a well-lit, airy, and spacious great room, with wide wood planks underfoot. High overhead wood beams and a brick arch separate the dining and seating areas from the kitchen. The Barn and an exercise building line up as the lower part of the L-shaped compound. Large, arched French-style barn doors on overhead sliders open the Barn on either side, for either privacy or shared family living.

An evolution of cheerful paint colors over the years has expressed an ongoing passion for the house. The interiors have an unusual palette of muted greens, pinks, and blues, developed from the original colors found in the Cottage. Regional craftsmen, many descendants of the original German settlers, executed the stonework, provided carpentry, and

forged hardware for doors and hinges in the same manner as their forefathers. Authenticity is revealed in every careful detail.

To bring the varied elements of the compound together, the architect used low limestone walls to define areas of the connecting buildings. The walls were also a reference to the stacked stone used by the German settlers as large enclosures around their gardens and fields. The entire compound is surrounded by another wall that defines the baby Bermuda grasses planted on the inside "lawns" from the hayfield and wild landscape beyond. The grasses go dormant to tolerate drought and happily revive when the rains come.

ABOVE: A table adjacent to the living and dining areas inside the Barn.

RIGHT: The great gathering room is furnished to accommodate large groups of family and friends. The iron chandelier was made in Italy in the mid-1800s.

ABOVE: The high-beamed ceilings and large armoire hint at the Cottage's cultural history. Bare stone floors and walls and limestone window frames create a monastic grace around a painted table.

RIGHT: The loft bedroom in the Cottage features a bistro table with chair and a seventeenth-century Spanish gilded wrought-iron bed.

OPPOSITE: A Sister Cottage interior: the living room and bedroom are downstairs, with loft dressing room and bath above.

Ramshorn Ranch, *Texas*

Ranches often begin as a small stone or wood building or human shelter. Gradually, success brings more cattle, leading to another building, perhaps a family for the rancher, an addition to the little house. Equipment means yet another shed, and then the big barn is built. A ranch is a series of moieties held together by necessity. The site plan for the Ramshorn Ranch is a variation on the thematic tribal or "pod" arrangement of buildings.

At the top of a thirsty, sun-absorbing mesa, on land the family held in ownership for more than twenty years, Joey and Ed Story wanted to build a house larger than the small cabin that had been their

getaway. The site is crowded with rock outcroppings, shaded intermittently by the perpetually lovely oaks of the Hill Country. The Texas landscape and the 360-degree views of the Gaudalupe River Valley deserved a unique approach to western life.

BELOW: The exterior of the master bedroom pod and its connection to the great room and large covered limestone porch with outdoor ovens.

RIGHT: The thirty-foot-diameter reflecting pool was built to resemble an animal water trough. The three pods of limestone and metal are the great room to the right, the kitchen, and master bedroom.

"At the top in the center was this place where you would go and build a fire, enjoy the views, and watch the weather change. We thought that was the perfect site for the house," explains architect Ted Flato. An old cabin had been a shepherd's shack near a small goat shed.

A circular plan would bring the best views from the hilltop. The idea of separate buildings gathered loosely around a thirty-foot water pool made it into the final plan. Since the site has no live water source, the idea of the courtyard plan encircling the pool was well received. The pool is a raised watering trough for the animals and an anchor for the other buildings.

Rough-cut local limestone and galvanized metal make up the five buildings that are linked around the reflecting pool. The buildings are all perfect squares,

with the exception of the great room, which is a large rectangle. The largest structure is a series of three smaller, hipped-roof buildings. The residence was planned as a compound of buildings arranged in and out of an oak copse on the hill, taking advantage of the rock outcroppings in the landscape for dramatic perspectives. The main building houses the great room, with its large fireplace and dining area. Both spaces are enveloped by floor-to-ceiling windows. Interior woodwork in the great room is Texas long-leaf pine and soft fir, although the twenty-foot-high, vaulted, temple-style ceiling is constructed of Douglas fir. The owners wanted a layered wood above the living room and of simple construction. "Every piece of timber is a supporting piece and a true expression of the structure," says Ted Flato. "Nothing is for show." Angled slightly from the living and dining areas is the kitchen bar, where "saddle up" is literal—the bar stools are saddles that face the activities of the cooking area. Divided from the great room by

PREVIOUS PAGES: The gravel road down the hill past the pond and an old oak tree.

BELOW: Dining under the covered porch with 360-degree views of the countryside.

OPPOSITE: The wood temple roof of the living and dining rooms complements the limestone walls and concrete floors. The furnishings were collected by the owners on their global travels.

ABOVE: Branch and pony-hide furniture in the study.

ABOVE RIGHT: Navajo blankets and western chaps are vintage pieces.

RIGHT: A fringed pillow and chairs are part of the owner's western collection.

OPPOSITE: Items collected in Thailand, Mongolia, and Singapore.

the bar, the cooking area becomes its own structure. A door in the kitchen leads to a pod housing the master bedroom, bath, and dressing room.

Landscaping was blended into the natural-growth surroundings. An exterior stone path covered with a pergola of heavy peeled cedar branches and flush with vines unifies the three buildings and creates nooks, gardening tables, and private spaces around the perimeter under the flowering arbor. The house is home to a collection of animals: Sicilian donkeys, koi, horses, and dogs.

The compound is inseparable from its geography, nestled naturally into its landscape. The great room opens at the far end onto a beautifully land-scaped area of covered ripple stone (quarried from the floor of a river) and a pergola court dominated by three stone piers that bear the forces of the slop-ing shed roof. A massive stone fireplace, a wood-burning barbecue and pizza oven, combined with nearby cabinet counters, completes the amenities for dining al fresco. The oak-carpeted hills can be seen from every compass point.

Across the courtyard opposite the reflecting pool are two additional sixteen-foot square structures. One is a study, which is furnished in a Western tradi-tion with artifacts such as Navajo weavings, horn carvings, cherished silverwork. Books, photographs, and cowboy arts were acquired with dedication to regional works and the consultation of a regional specialist. The study is linked to the other building, a guest bedroom, by a metal-clad guest bath. Each space has a private porch, a standing seam galva-nized room, and a "lifetime roof," lasting fifty to seventy-five years. Many of the floors are a soft, smooth unstained concrete, revealing a mottled finish, a nod to the outlying dappled landscape.

Star Creek Ranch, *Texas*

A stalwart Irish adventurer, Peter Gallagher was one of the first immigrants to ride into the Fredericksburg hills. He rode from San Antonio and turned northwest early one afternoon. Late in the afternoon of the next day, he topped a rise to see spread out before him the purple ridge lines of mountains in silhouette, before a red setting sun. The Edenic valley of the San Geronimo River flowed with streams, deep canyons, and rugged hills.

In the 1850s this part of Texas was being settled by people of French, German, Irish, English, and Hispanic ancestry. The Southern Texas classical idiom may not have been as random as is often thought. Early settlers innately brought classical proportion to their work, as do immigrants to every country.

The land was a prairie of sloping hills scattered with live oaks, rivers, streams, and narrow riparian pecan bottoms. Today, rivers and streams are concealed among the oak canopies that grow so close together they overtake the dips and turns of the small valleys and low hills. There are no distant vistas here: the landscape is personal; an intimate and private garden. A rushing stream or a body of clear, still,

water is often edged with an undercut of low granite canyon walls, themselves thick with maidenhair ferns.

Diane and Jack Gotcher made a promise to each other to live on land near the place they spent their first anniversary. They celebrated their twenty-fifth wedding anniversary the year they bought the

LEFT: A curtained and shaded dining terrace overlooks the rockscape and pool.

RIGHT: A granite Star Creek sign and stone path lead to the front door.

ranch in the Hill Country. They first built a small, limestone-faced house in the traditional style of the area, using rectangular, cut rock. The double-rock walls had cut rock on the exterior and field rock on the interior. The interior rock, never intended to be exposed, was plastered over. Today, an exposed rock interior is highly prized, and homestead walls are undergoing plaster removal to reveal the natural stone wall underneath.

Inspired by log cabin and barn architecture, Diane had a vision that would bring together the indigenous forms in their country home. They had attempted to draw plans in which an old barn might have existed on the property and received later additions. It was an intricate and complicated project that would be sited on a small ledge along the edge of a creek. Undaunted, Diane gathered old building parts with the help of a person who sold log cabins. Her boundless vision and perseverance wrangled such artifacts as barn sections, corn cribs, a set of double-crib log barns, a single log cabin, and a rock schoolhouse, all of which are incorporated, along with the small limestone house, into her unique vision of ranch history.

OPPOSITE LEFT: Double entry doors open to the front path and porches.

OPPOSITE RIGHT: Delicate patio peach blooms in troughs above the pool and garden stream below.

LEFT: A private corner for outdoor dining.

BELOW: Willy and Ernie stop by.

rock for this thin layer of flooring before the operation closed.

The fireplace is the major decorative element that separates the living and dining areas. The design was inspired by photos of an old Adirondack lodge in upstate New York. This one, however, was built from the stone steps of an old Texas church, reclaimed chimney rock from Comanche County, and rubble rock from the Gotcher property that had been piled up years and years ago while the fields on the other side of their creek were being cleared. As the story goes, local settlers' children never told their parents

The main part of the house is a voluminous barn-style area. It is configured in large sections of a living space and dining room, divided by a floor-to-roof fireplace. An upper loft, kitchen, and nook are all under the main barn roof. The rock wall separating the barn from the kitchen is twenty-four inches thick. Vignette areas for privacy and reading fill the perimeter of the larger spaces. The double-rock walls in the barn area are 19^1/$_2$″ thick. Under the Vermont barn roof are white pine barn posts, planks, and beams, some of which are twenty-four inches wide. The floors below are clad with Texas limestone from a quarry on a private ranch in central Texas that was able to quarry just enough

that they had nothing to do, because the parents
would send them to the fields to pick up rocks.

The balance of the house is a collection of the
farm, school, and ranch buildings that are designed
as bedrooms and guest rooms. The old rock schoolhouse from Long Cove, Texas, has twenty-inch-thick
double-rock walls. The two-room schoolhouse is
large enough for one of the classrooms to accommodate the graceful 19½-by-27-foot-long master
bath and dressing room. A limestone addition to the
fireplace leaves the shower and vanity areas secluded
at the end of the space. The bathtub is concrete with
copper fixtures.

The Gotchers live at Star Creek full time, with
the demands of their ranch life including feeding the
longhorns, whitetail deer, albino catfish, and birds.
They have hundreds of acres to tend and a field of
thousands of wildflowers, including Texas bluebonnets, Indian blanket, Missouri primrose, lazy daisy,
prairie coneflower, winecups, and Mexican hat. In
autumn, flameleaf sumac turns bright red; little
bluestem and bushy bluestem turn orange-red. Cedar
elms turn a brilliant yellow. The big pecan bottom
plays host to chuck-wagon cookouts, parties, and
grandchildren pitching tents in the shade.

LEFT: The large double doors and foyer lead to the entry stairs of the living area, whose entry echoes the front doors. A large dining room is on the other side of the stone fireplace. The room was made from the remnants of a Vermont barn and posts that rise nearly thirty feet to the ceiling.

RIGHT: This bath has stone rubble resurrected from an old schoolhouse. On the other side of the limestone fireplace are recessed showers and vanities.

ABOVE: The walls of the card room came from double-crib log cabins.

OPPOSITE: A small wood fireplace in the kitchen can be used for baking breads; the island offers plenty of workspace.

LEFT: The master bedroom is another room from the old schoolhouse. A fireplace warms the sitting area at the end of the room.

ABOVE: A bedroom vignette; the mirror reflects the sitting area of the master suite.

RIGHT: The guest room features a child's bed at the foot of the iron bed frame. A child's cow-horn chair sits beside the doorway.

Cíbolo Creek Ranch, *Texas*

Cíbolo Creek is a thirty-thousand-acre working cattle ranch with one of the largest purebred longhorn herds in the United States. Situated in the Big Bend Country of far West Texas, among the Chinati Mountains on the Mexican border, the rugged terrain of rocky peaks, sheltered canyons, and mesas rises from four thousand to six thousand feet in elevation. The higher slopes are dotted with oak, juniper, and Mexican walnut trees. Cottonwoods, desert willows, and Arizona ash trees abound along the canyon floors and near the many springs. The ranch is crowned with many varieties of colorful mountain cactus species.

The Spanish word *cíbolo* is usually translated as "buffalo," which together with native elk and wild turkey have been reintroduced on the ranch. Camels, of the type used by the U.S. Calvary in the Big Bend Country in the nineteenth century, also have returned. Due to the mountainous terrain, the ranch has a large *remuda* of horses, mules, and burros to work the cattle and keep up the remote fence lines. Mountain lions, coyotes, javelinas, foxes, white-tailed and western mule deer, eagles, ducks, owls, doves, and quail are frequently spotted, and black bears are making a comeback.

The most remarkable features of the Big Bend are three adobe forts erected near three prolific springs on the property of the ranch. These fortifications were constructed by Big Bend pioneer

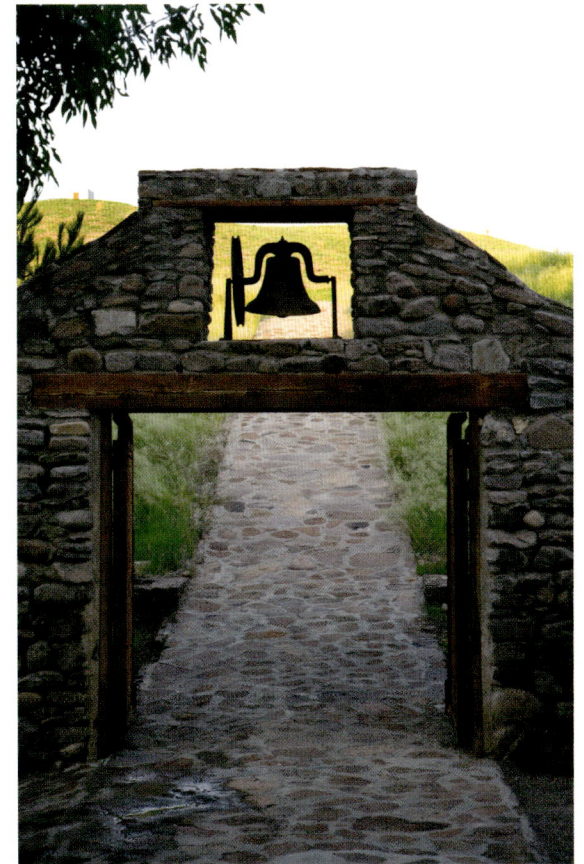

LEFT: Stone original to the property was restacked to divide the hacienda from the old fort and courtyard.

ABOVE: A stone and wood gate and bell tower at Cíbolo Creek Ranch.

Milton Faver in the 1850s within the valleys of the remote Chinatis, a range that was the stronghold of hostile Apaches near the Comanche Trail. The Great Spring of the Cíbolo lies in a narrow pass of considerable military and commercial significance at the foot of some of the highest peaks of the Chinati Mountains. This spring has provided water, without fail, for thousands of years. The abundance of ancient Indian artifacts attests to its importance.

Milton Faver acquired the title to Cíbolo spring and built the first of his three forts in 1857, possibly upon the remains of a Spanish mission settlement of the Cíbolo Indians that was founded in 1715. The state structure, El Fortín del Cíbolo, took the form of a quadrangular fortress with two round towers twenty feet in height, walls that were three feet thick, and a massive gate fabricated of large, rough-hewn beams. The fort measured 90 by 160 feet. Faver constructed his second fort immediately following the Civil War. El Fortín de la Ciénega, the "Fort of the Marsh," was built downstream from the fine Ciénega spring. Shortly after the completion of La Ciénega, El Fortín de la Morita, at the site of the beautiful

BELOW: The corner of the adobe fort El Fortín de la Morita, the Northeast tower.

RIGHT: A view of El Fortín del Cíbolo, the southeast tower facade.

BELOW RIGHT: Restacked stone walls and a protective grate over the window.

Morita spring, was built. La Ciénega is constructed in a square, as is La Morita. El Cíbolo is nearly twice the size of the smaller two.

From the outlying areas of El Paso to the hills far east of the Pecos River, Faver's outposts were the only substantial Anglo-American or Hispanic border settlements north of the Rio Grande that were not abandoned. A considerable portion of his livestock was lost, but Faver and his followers held on until the return of the Union forces in 1867.

ABOVE: The interior courtyard of El Fortín del Cíbolo.

The Indian and bandit attacks continued sporadically, but nothing stopped Faver from his return to prosperity. The rigors of frontier life eventually caught up with the—by that time exhausted, yet honored—"Don Melitón," who passed away in 1889, leaving the estate to his wife, Francisca, and his only child, Juan. Juan died in 1913, followed shortly by his mother. Sadly, Cíbolo Creek Ranch passed through several owners over the years and finally succumbed to picturesque ruin prior to its purchase by John Poindexter in 1990 and the start of a historic restoration.

The restoration plan for the three fortresses that once defended Don Melitón's territory was to maintain their historical authenticity, from the hand-tied *ocotillo* roofs to the hand-forged hardware. The first phase was the rebuilding of the adobes. Chris Carson, senior partner of the San Antonio architectural firm of Ford, Powell and Carson, delivered the

OPPOSITE: The sapling and squared timber roof of the courtyard of El Fortín del Cíbolo.

RIGHT: Abandoned rooms of sanctuary and artifacts.

plans for El Fortín del Cíbolo. The sizable restored structure, including the area devoted to a flagstone courtyard and porch, measured 6,280 square feet from the exterior surfaces of the thick walls.

Don Melitón had possessed no door or window glass at such remote a site as El Fortín del Cíbolo, so the architectural design included a number of ingenious features. Using a series of photographs as a guide, two sets of double-leaf doors were designed; the outer double doors were placed on pivots and rotate 180 degrees—90 degrees in each direction from the closed position. A second set of double doors, also operating on pivots, incorporated glass panes in place of traditional wood panels. The gates, doors, windows, and trim that appeared in photographs were reproduced and sanded to convey the impression of age. In order to enter a room, one must step over a barrier about six inches in height, which in earlier times impeded the inflow of cold winter air.

The purpose of the contemporary hacienda at El Cíbolo is to isolate in a separate but adjoining building the functions that would be in conflict with the tone of the old fort. Thus, the hacienda houses a large kitchen, the screened veranda, entertaining and

dining spaces, twelve bedrooms, and various service areas. The Hispanic tone of the hacienda was enhanced by the use of smooth Saltillo tile, in three sizes, on the floors. Hand-painted and glazed Mexican Talavera tiles were used in dressing, bath, and kitchen locations. Brass fixtures are of a restrained design suggestive of an earlier time and are consistent with the hacienda style. The interior spaces in the fort provide a formal dining room, a library and museum, an expansive living room suite, and intimate areas for conversation and reading. A new stone fence divides the new hacienda from the old fort and defines the path of the main courtyard. Taken together, the old and new structures incorporate all of the functions needed for life and work in the Big Bend Country.

ABOVE: The Texas sunset over the hills and Lake Cíbolo.

RIGHT: Deck chairs on the stone terrace at the lake.

Historical artifacts are displayed throughout El Fortín del Cíbolo, representative of the Big Bend, the Mexican border, and the Cíbolo Creek Ranch. These items were collected from individual contributors, specialty merchants, vendors of military equipment and apparel, antiques dealers, and private collections. The screened veranda and horse tack room of the hacienda are furnished with Mexican furniture, while the hacienda living room, like the master suite, is decorated in the southwestern style.

LEFT: One of the restored rooms, including the adobe walls and furnishings, at the La Ciénega fort at Cíbolo Creek Ranch.

BELOW: The doorway to the *Los Santos* guest room with a name plaque.

OPPOSITE: The large dining room with *vigas-y-raja* ceiling, adobe walls, and doors that open onto the sun-filled terrace.

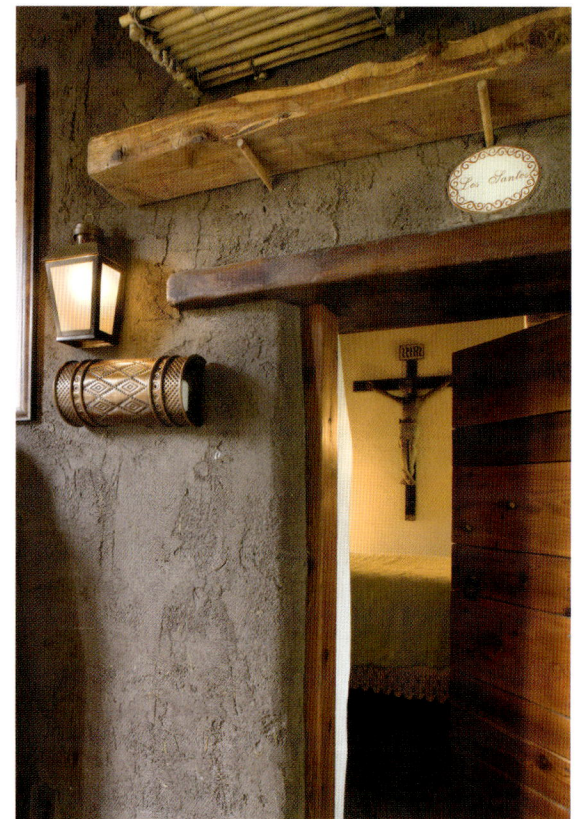

The first room of the north tower is the ranch library, with approximately 750 volumes. The walls are clad with reproductions of ranch titles, patents, asset transference, and other official documents. The first floor of the northwest tower contains a collection of more than five hundred Indian artifacts. Other Indian items include jewelry, stone implements, woven materials, and bow strings.

The fort courtyard near the old stone corral is where the larger historical items are found. Many old benches, oil urns, wood and stone watering troughs, and a carpenter's bench hold history in their power. The iron wagon-wheel rims and Mexican cart wheels are propped against the fort and corral walls, where four antique wagons and carts have come to rest.

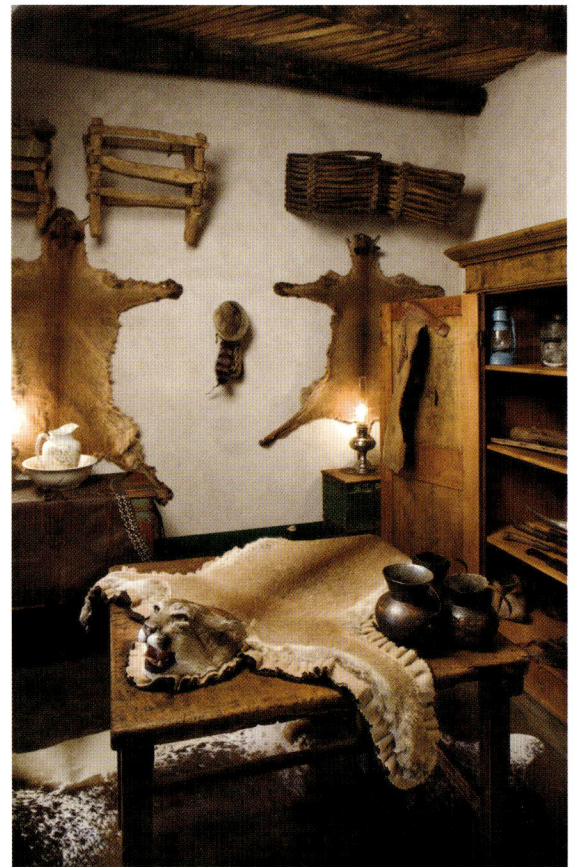

LEFT: Stone floors, adobe walls, *vigas* ceiling in the library, and stairs to the tower.

ABOVE: A room of artifacts and wild game trophy hides.

OPPOSITE LEFT: A guest room with an antique Spanish and Mexican bed, and floor and upholstery weavings. Saltillo tiles were used on the floor.

OPPOSITE RIGHT: A guest room with carved bed, horse, and *fogón* fireplace.

UTAH

B

NAVAJOS

A INDIANS

San Bernardo

Taos

Cordova

INDIANS

Embudo

Albiquiu

Joya

Luceros

San Juan

Cachuti

Chama

Canada

Sierra de Tunecha

River de Chelly

SANTA

SANTA FE

Ft. R

Sierra de Chuses

Washington Pass

Simpson Trail

FE

Pecos

Ft. Defiance

Jemes

SA

N

Rio Puerco

S. Felipe

Puerto

Galisteo

Galisteo

C. Mi

OQUIS

Campbells Pass

Bernalillo

Laguna

INDIANS

Crater

S Mateo M

Corrales

S. Pedro

El Whipple 1854

Rio de Zuñi

ALBUQUERQUE

Zuni

L

5.035

6.824

S. Antonio

Zuñi Pass

Laguna

Atrisco

Placeres

Pajarito

Padillas

Isleta

Lunas

Peralta

Valencia

Capt. Sitgreaves 1852

Belen

St. James

C

MEXICO

Sabina

Joya de Cibaletta

M

Little Colorado Chiquito R.

Burnt Fork

E

X

Joyita

I

O

Poladera

Sabino

Lamitar

Parida

Scorro

Mts

O

R

L. Lopez

Don Pedro

R

Valverde

El Contral

Fra Cristobal

Salina de San Andres

Aztec

Valley

Gold Mines

Capt by Maj. Emory

APACHES

INDIANS

Ojo del Muerto

L. Del Muerto

N

O

Santa Barbara

Copper Mines

N

by W. E. Smith 1849

Part V: *New Mexico and California*

"The charm of the very primitive and early Mexican, New Mexican and Pueblo adobe structures…their projecting vigas *extended unevenly because it was difficult and laborious to cut them off evenly…also spaced unevenly because the builders had no rulers. The plastering, if any, was a coating of lime or clay, whitewashed, and was merely a method of covering the adobes for protection, the result being delightful because the finish coat followed the undulating surface beneath in a natural fashion." (John Byers,* The Influence of Adobe in California, A Traditional Adaptation, *1929).*

The Bell Ranch, *New Mexico*

The Bell Ranch lies in an untouched landscape of grasslands, mesas, canyons, and buttes in the north-eastern part of New Mexico. The Canadian River, Conchas Lake, and La Cinta Creek all provide fresh water. A beautiful, bell-shaped mountain and a variety of distinctive land features stand apart in this austere climate.

The area encompassing the Bell Ranch was granted by Mexico to Don Pablo Montoya in 1824, long before New Mexico became a U.S. territory (1850) and achieved statehood (1912). John S. Watts, a Santa Fe attorney, gained control of the property in 1864, and the U.S. government confirmed the title. Wilson Waddingham, a real estate and mining baron from Canada, brought cattle to the ranch in

BELOW: A *latilla*-style fence outside the lawns and terrace of the White House, which dates to the mid-1800s and houses sleeping and living quarters, the manager's residence, and cooking quarters.

RIGHT: The main gate to the Hacienda on the Bell Ranch property.

1872 and registered the Bell brand in 1874. A group of New York investors owned the Bell from 1894 to 1899, then shareholders of the Red River Valley Company owned the ranch until 1947. Harriet E. Keeney owned the ranch headquarters and approximately 130,000 acres until the sale to William N. Lane in 1970. During his tenure, Lane

later built the "Hacienda" to bring the ranch to its current size.

The Bell consists of 250,000 deeded, blocked acres stemming from the Don Pablo Montoya Mexican land grant of 1824. The absence of state lands within the Bell's borders provides a vast private land holding in the West. The western portion

ABOVE: The patio inside the *latilla* fence. Chairs sit under shade trees in front of the manager's residence.

UPPER RIGHT: The vernacular architecture of the White House with screened porch and shade trees protecting the yard from the afternoon sun.

LOWER RIGHT: The long, dusty roads in the distance and the reddish rocks and desert.

of the ranch is bisected by the Canadian River, which creates its own landscape and habitat. The central portion of the ranch is predominantly open grassland with a variety of browse and grasses making up the heart of the livestock range. The vista is broken by Bell Mountain, Huerfano Mesa, and Gavilan Mesa. The eastern portion of the ranch offers grass and brush habitat in canyon lands consisting of cedar and ponderosa pine. The contrasting landscapes offer a variety of habitats for diverse populations of wildlife, including mule deer, white-tail deer, antelope, turkey, blue quail, dove, and waterfowl.

The Bell's buildings offer both historical and functional structures for use by the ranch hands and owners. The Hacienda, which serves as the owner's residence and guest lodge, is a large, Spanish-style structure on the north end of the ranch near the head of La Cinta Creek. Built in the 1930s by Guy Waggoner, a prior owner of part of the Bell Ranch, the Hacienda has historical significance and was visited over the years by such Hollywood stars as Clark Gable, Roy Rogers, Dale Evans, and Howard Hughes, who would fly in for hunting and social festivities. The Hacienda is meticulously landscaped and overlooks the heart of the Bell Ranch, with

views of Bell Mountain and Huerfano Mesa. Eight bedrooms are located in its east and west wings and have external access to the courtyard, outdoor pool, and tennis court. A casino/recreation building and two separate homes compose the balance of the Hacienda complex. Four ranch camps in outlying areas serve as homes for ranch hands, allowing them to care for livestock in various parts of the property, which has five hundred miles of roads.

The "Headquarters" lies along La Cinta Creek and includes the White House, which dates to the mid-1800s. It has a regional vernacular design, with simple whitewashed walls, dust-blue shutters, and a sloping roof of reddish galvanized metal. The center courtyard features a triangular patio made of flat desert stone and a long, green lawn enclosed within a low fence of *latillas* (saplings) and a barn-red gate. The White House accommodates the manager's residence in the west wing, a middle section of sleeping quarters, and separate living quarters in the east wing. The cookhouse, office, and cook's quarters are contained in a separate structure in the middle of the Headquarters complex. A typical ranch hand arrives at the Bell cookhouse or one of the four camps at five in the morning (sometimes earlier on hot summer days), for breakfast and the orders for the day delivered from the cow boss. Three separate homes, the historic barn, corrals, and miscellaneous outbuildings make up the balance of the complex.

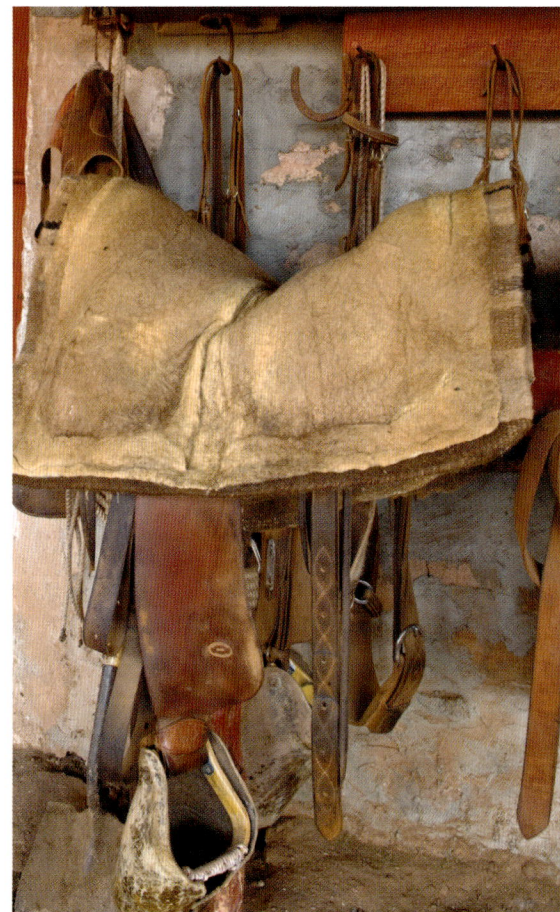

OPPOSITE: The Hacienda serves as the owner's residence and guest lodge.

ABOVE: The outdoor *fogón* near the covered patio for outdoor fires.

ABOVE RIGHT: The Hacienda corridor to the swimming pool, with views of the Bell Mountain and Huerfano Mesa.

RIGHT: The shaded and cool depths of the loggia at the Hacienda.

PREVIOUS PAGES: The large party room is furnished with a fireplace, Spanish lamps and furniture, and several conversation areas. Built by Guy Waggoner, a prior owner, it was a favorite hangout for Clark Gable, Roy Rogers, Dale Evans, and Howard Hughes in the 1930s.

OPPOSITE: A dining space for many diners and guests in the party room.

ABOVE: The piano at the end of the party room. The kitchen and bar are at the right.

RIGHT: Many of the eight guest rooms feature *fogón* fireplaces, this one with brass andirons of cactus and figures.

LaPides Ranch, *New Mexico*

A mountainous terrain covered with kaleidoscopic wildflowers, this ranch land near Santa Fe is in the high desert. Owner Allene LaPides and her late husband, Jerome, discovered a lovely ranch where old buildings could be restored and a new home would be built. The abundant piñon trees blend with wild native shrubs and grasses that have renaturalized the sixty-acre property. One travels over rustic gravel roads and paths to the house, a route that takes visitors by surprise as the road emerges from the protective cover of trees and shrubs and becomes rolling hills, then pastures, and finally offers a glimpse of an eighteenth-century fountain. Sculptures appear throughout the tumbleweed and scrub. A small stream meanders through the property, where the animals graze beneath the shadows of the Sangre de Cristo Mountains.

The land was ideal for the LaPides, who had lived in a large house close to Allene LaPides's gallery, one of the preeminent galleries in Santa Fe. She represented contemporary artists who worked in oils, photography, sculpture, *retablos*, bronzes, and glass. Quirky mixes of media and style filled her collection. Her artists included Peter Beard, Ida Kohlmeyer,

LEFT: Colorful tumbled stone pavers and sage shrubs fill the approach to the distant main gate, with sculpture in the foreground.

Al Held, Alex Katz, Bruce Nauman, and her own nephew, Herb Ritts. Eventually the gallery space was too small for the growing business, and she arranged for the Georgia O'Keeffe collection to move in. The space is now the new Georgia O'Keeffe Museum.

To design her New Mexico home, LaPides hired the Texas-based firm Three Architecture (designers of her favorite hotel, the Peninsula in Beverly Hills), who worked closely with Los Angeles–based interior designer Martyn Lawrence-Bullard. The expansive, eleven-thousand-square-foot, one-bedroom ranch house was built in the traditional adobe style, with walls more than two feet thick, as LaPides maintained a commitment to the integrity of traditional indigenous building techniques. The design requirements were not typical, for the owner wished to have a nonlinear interior plan. Rooms were to be offset from one another in an unconventional manner befitting

the movement and activities of her daily life. As in traditional southwestern Spanish design, there are views from room to room and around corners. The surrounding grounds have four guest cabins, a barn, a twenty-horse stable, and an indoor arena, all of which harmonize perfectly with the regional atmosphere.

The interiors of the house are a blend of Lawrence-Bullard's appreciation for European furnishings and the styling of the Portuguese estate. The ceilings are beamed with rugged, refinished railroad ties spaced in tight intervals. The enormous beams challenge the loftiness of the light-filled rooms

ABOVE: The entry gate among floral borders.

RIGHT: A horse with eye protection in the state-of-the-art stables.

BELOW: A brass door handle detail.

and the softness of the floors. In the main public room, the fireplaces were built with seventeenth- and eighteenth-century Italian stone. The floors were paved in a random, offset pattern of antique French limestone to achieve a feeling of relaxed elegance.

The eighteenth-century Italian and Portuguese furnishings selected by the designer are meant to anchor the extraordinary collection of contemporary art. Lawrence-Bullard chose antique Portuguese tables and chests, Spanish iron chandeliers, and rare Indian and French antique textiles. Natural materials

such as raw silk and jute borders emphasize the simplicity of this highly sophisticated design. The Orangery, a two-story interior well topped by a skylight, incorporates an antique tile fresco of eighteenth-century Spanish horses in the Portuguese style.

The Allene and Jerome LaPides Foundation, based in Santa Fe, is dedicated to animal welfare, child welfare, women's issues, the environment, and arts education for youth. The ranch has become the forever home to numerous rescued animals, including many horses that will live out their days here.

LEFT: An intersection of spaces. The dining area is on the right.

BELOW: On the left is the foyer and covered patio. Furnishings are by Martyn Lawrence-Bullard.

ABOVE: The sunroom.

RIGHT: The owner wanted to be able to see many rooms from one perspective. Here the view is toward the main living and dining area.

OPPOSITE: The antique marquetry dining table with orchids; a painted bookcase is in the background.

ABOVE: A collection of boxes and books.

RIGHT: The fireplace and enthusiastic wall color.

ABOVE: An antique secretary and globe; a sepia print is on the wall.

BELOW: Herb Ritts's *Darati, Profile, Africa*, 1993, mounted in the foyer.

RIGHT: The entry foyer and gallery open to the kitchen, living room, and dining area.

Santa Ynez Valley Ranch, *California*

The stagecoach line ran through the Santa Ynez Valley as early as 1858 from San Francisco to Yuma, Arizona. This valley had always been thought of as cowboy country. Land, overlooked for generations, was inexpensive. The oak-speckled, inland valley ranges and savannas were perceived as good only for cattle and farming. But the soil was rich, and the farmers of the region did well with such exotic crops as olives, quince, and almonds. Soon crops in the valley aroused the interest of people who wished to grow wine on a moderate scale. Today, wine grapes, from which hundreds of handcrafted artisanal wines are made, reflect the finest characteristics of the valley vineyards.

The Santa Ynez Valley ranches of today are still home to cattle and horses. Young animals coltishly romp through the high grasses of this blissful valley located west of coastal Santa Barbara, California. The panoramic terrain has a lush quality that is ideal for the combination of modest-sized ranches and large, old, family landholdings. The climate of the region is conducive to breeding thoroughbreds, and the area is known nationally for its horse expertise. The semi-arid landscape is scattered with live oaks, red and white oaks, sagebrush, black sage, purple needlegrass, coyote bush, cacti, yarrow, and California poppies.

LEFT: A California ranch courtyard is furnished for twilight.

This seductive Santa Ynez Valley ranch is located on a rocky knoll overlooking natural grassland. Framed by the Santa Ynez Mountains, the property is one hundred acres of vast pastureland and hills, with the purple silhouettes of mountains in the distance. The approach to the ranch house is by way of a private road, which leads to the auto-court. A thick plaster wall punctuated by large wooden doors grants entry to the main courtyard, designed for outdoor living on verandas and numerous porches. An outside fireplace is the center of an intimate gathering space near an exterior stairway leading up to the tower. The courtyard offers access to different bedrooms and other rooms inside, as well as to the kitchen. An east terrace has views of the south valley toward the Santa Ynez Mountains and overlooks a portion of the ranch where animals graze. The vast pastures maintain an intimacy due to the low mountains beyond a one-acre pond created in the small valley below the house. Amid native water plants, a bridge crosses the pond to a path leading to the ranch office located out of view of the main residence.

The house was designed using conventional wood-frame construction. Double framing was used for the thick-walled adobe structure. The owner chose metal-frame casement windows and doors, similar to those used in the 1930s. The roof is a flat pan tile, which traces to a time when European architecture had some influence on Spanish design.

On the porches, wood sheathing was spaced so that the bottom of the tile was exposed. The house has plaster surfaces on the inside, as well as on the exterior. Simple raised plaster trim details were added at the eaves and ceilings. Around some of the openings, precast concrete trim was added. Integral color was added to the plaster, and a soft hand-

ABOVE: The distant beauty of the hills that divided the valley from Santa Barbara on the coast.

RIGHT: The horse barn is camouflaged by the trees, grasses, and hills below the house.

OPPOSITE TOP: The barn stalls, guesthouse, and riding corral.

OPPOSITE BOTTOM: Horses in the pasture in the foothills.

UPPER RIGHT: A horse getting prepared for grooming.

LOWER RIGHT: The interior of the horse barn and stalls.

FOLLOWING PAGES: Breakfast in the sun.

plaster texture was used. The corners of the plaster were shaped by hand.

Recycled products were used. The owner salvaged all the interior doors and beams from other buildings. Most were used in an "as-is condition," giving the house a rustic patina. The ceiling of the tower room was painted dark blue with gold stairs. The floors are glazed concrete with black inset stone patterns in some places, wide-plank oak wood in others, and Saltillo tile over the raised floor portions. Five fireplaces have a Rumsford design with an exposed herringbone brick pattern. Each chimney cap has a different combination of flat tile, barrel tile, and plaster.

The owner grew up in Washington State and purchased the ranch from Ellen DeGeneres, who had recently renovated the house and furnished the interiors. No alterations were needed. One of the owner's favorite places is the gazebo, with views of the mountains, the pond, and the pastures. Another favorite pastime is watching cattle and horses graze. This is a nonworking ranch, and the livestock here are treasured pets.

LEFT: The concrete floor with a stone pattern, leather sling-back chairs, and fireplace evoke the original California ranches.

BELOW: The bright interiors of the open dining room and kitchen spaces are delineated by the patterns of the Saltillo tiles and borders. The harvest table and red leather chairs are old California pieces.

OPPOSITE: Four sets of French doors fill the living room with light.

LEFT: The master bedroom features a raised-hearth fireplace and built-in window seat. The small stools are used for books. The headboard niche is used for flowering plants.

ABOVE: The guest room with attached balcony and bath.

The Diamond A Ranch,
New Mexico

Diamond A Ranch is a one-hundred-thousand-acre property in Lincoln County, New Mexico. Fed by the waters of the Hondo River, the land is an unexpected oasis of poplar trees and orchards in the barren foothills of the Capitan Mountains in the south-central part of the state. The Capitan Mountain range is about twenty miles long and six miles wide, formed from large, elongated granite shelves. It is the only mountain range in North America that runs east to west, and the Spanish settlers used its unnamed peak, which rises more than ten thousand feet, as a landmark. It is said that on their way to and from Santa Fe, they buried Spanish treasure in some of the numerous caves throughout the mountains.

The original Diamond A homestead dates from the nineeenth century, a flamboyant period of outlaws and cattle barons versus bankers and merchants that finally led to what is known as the Lincoln County War. Today, the owners, Mr. and Mrs. Gerald J. Ford, maintain three thousand sheep, four hundred cattle, forty horses, and one hundred acres of unharvested apple orchards. The main house on the property was built in 1964 to the drawings and specifications of Herbert Bayer, an abstract

painter who was Walter Gropius's favorite student at the Bauhaus. The facades, with their great two-story porches, loosely reproduced one of the masterpieces of Territorial-style architecture, the Baca House in Upper Las Vegas, New Mexico. Two older structures were also incorporated into the design: a humble Territorial-style cottage north of the front lawn (now guest quarters) and the Adobe Wing, a historic building that once served as a way station on the stagecoach route from Lincoln to Roswell, stretch-

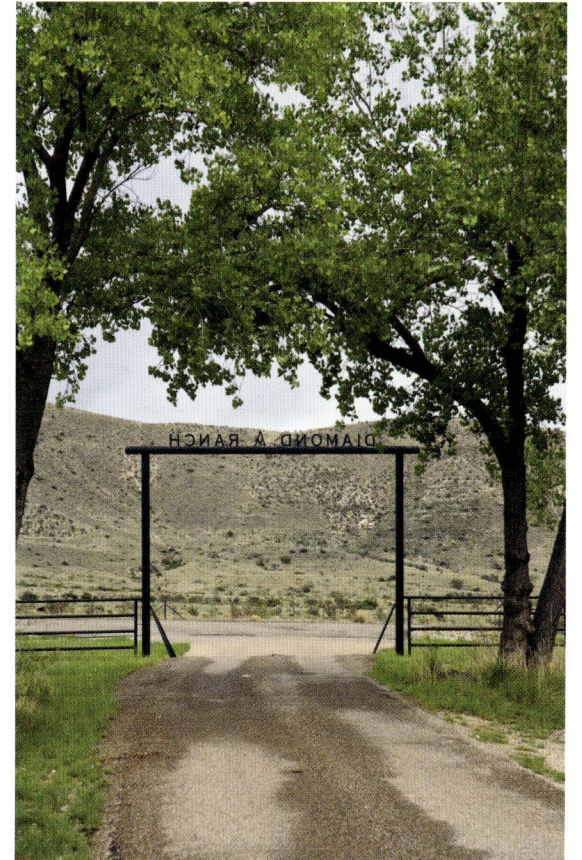

LEFT: A barn style used in the east with cupolas. Used for hay storage, the structure is placed on the ridgeline for ventilation.

ing toward the east. Three additional buildings were soon added to the compound: a freestanding chapel, where Bayer's abstract modernism is softened by a Baroque portal and campanile salvaged from the ruins of a seventeenth-century Mexican church; a skylit indoor pool pavilion that is punctuated with several sets of French doors leading to the outdoor lawns and features rather wan Victorian details; and a large, freestanding structure housing an impressive

Jacobean library paneled in Irish oak. The paneling was salvaged from the turn-of-the-century Huntington Mansion in Hillsborough, California, but some of it, including the mantel's fanciful carved figures of American Indians, dates to the late sixteenth century.

Peter Pennoyer Architects of New York undertook the delicate restoration of this architectural treasure. In the intervening years the interiors and the Adobe Wing deteriorated into lackluster bits of

ABOVE: The two-story main house with its famed long porches was built in 1964 to the specifications of abstract painter Herbert Bayer.

work, the wing becoming a "rabbit warren of tiny bedrooms." The attic of the main house had been used as a vast, ski lodge–style A-frame meant to display modern art, and the parlors and bedrooms below it were stark and boxy. "The haphazard growth of the complex also meant that the landscape is ill-defined, that it was difficult to move from one wing of the house to another, and also it was difficult to entertain on a large scale," says the architect.

Pennoyer decided to unify the Adobe Wing, the pool pavilion, the main house, and the library with a new, stone-flagged patio lined on three sides by a traditional New Mexican portal. The patio, a typical feature in Spanish- and Texas-style residences, serves as a focus for outdoor entertaining. To the north, a new wing of the house contains a forty-foot-long living room and, on the second floor, the master suite. East of the patio is a new bar. Lined in studded leather panels and with an oak ceiling, it echoes—without

replicating—the form and scale of the Jacobean library beyond. The original library was restored to perfection and given a new ceiling. To the west of the patio, the pool pavilion, thought to be a ballroom in the early 1840s and converted to a pool house in the 1920s, was rebuilt in the Greek revival style.

The restoration and redesign of the interiors incorporates influences from the successive stages of Lincoln County history. The eastern guest suite in the Adobe Wing was meticulously restored in old, traditional materials: mud floors, rich plaster

BELOW LEFT: The courtyard and patio fountain.

BELOW RIGHT: The main house showing the adobe wing.

RIGHT: The loggia of the courtyard with lunch table.

OPPOSITE: A wrought-iron gate and brick courtyard before the small ranch chapel.

RIGHT: A hand-carved stone door surround and the interior of the chapel.

walls textured with hay, and ceilings of *vigas* (logs) and *latillas* (saplings). The pool pavilion and the new living room and portal columns represent a brief efflorescence of the Greek revival in the 1840s, when New Mexico became a U.S. territory and the army engineers arrived from the east with their pattern books. The main house has tinted plaster walls that recall the days when the Territorial style of the 1860s began to metamorphose into a more rustic and provincial vernacular.

The master dressing suite and third-floor guest rooms are all tucked into gabled roofs and evoke an 1880s railroad style—the New Mexico variant of Queen Anne. The library, new bar, and dining room suggest the baronial eclecticism of the early twentieth century. Finally, the décor of the new living room represents one era superimposed on another: the Greek revival parlor has been revivified in the 1920s Pueblo revival style.

LEFT: The barrel ceiling in the dining room is covered with silk panels.

ABOVE: Leather wall panels are featured in the bar.

OPPOSITE: Deep wood paneling and coffered ceilings in the Jacobean library. Intricate carvings next to the marble fireplace surround and above the mantel include pedestals, faces, and dentils that rise up the medallion shields circling the base of the ceiling.

ABOVE: A saddle of significance graces the entry to the living room.

RIGHT: A collection of hand-tooled leather and silver-laden saddles.

ABOVE LEFT: A detail from a collection of silver spurs.

ABOVE RIGHT: The spur collection is behind glass on the right. The saddle collection fills the hallway.

LOWER LEFT: The interior of a guest room from the adobe wing.

LOWER RIGHT: A reflection in the antler mirror of the guest room.

Robledal Ranch, *California*

A smart yet uninhibited Irish immigrant by the name of Thomas W. Hope came to Texas during the Revolution in 1836 to become a cowboy. His adventures led him to the West Coast, where he first saw the beauty of Santa Barbara on the way to San Francisco, where he married. Hope and his wife raised enough money to buy two thousand sheep, which he, as a drover on horseback, moved down to Santa Barbara. There he leased land from the Cieneguitas Indians to provide grazing land for the herd.

During the Civil War, wool was in high demand, and Hope became wealthy. Although he never learned to read or write, he loved horses and purchased the spectacular six-thousand-acre Las Positas y Calera Ranch from a ranch widow. An exceptional inland freshwater lake, Laguna Blanca, sat at the center of what became known as the Hope Ranch. Pines and cypresses, along with hundreds of palm trees, were planted along the main entry and exit roads to help distinguish the ranch as a favorite weekend picnic and party location for the Hopes' many friends. Horse racing became a hobby when

Thomas put a horse track around Laguna Blanca. In time, wealthy estate properties began to appear and competed with the finest nearby Montecito homes and gardens. Acreage of the original Hope Ranch was sold for well-designed, smaller ranches.

George Washington Smith and Reginald Johnson, two of America's foremost architects, were the designers of the earliest estates built on the new Hope Ranch acreage. Smith was commissioned in 1928 to design Robledal Ranch for Milton Wilson,

LEFT: At the end of an oak-shaded road is the entrance to the Robledal Ranch motor court.

RIGHT: A detail of the garden and a small shed. The fountain is an Islamic star with mosaics, popular in Spanish architecture.

a partner in the Hope Ranch project. The name Robledal, meaning "an abundance of oaks," is derived from the landscape of low hills, ranges, and shallow valleys of old California that are covered with islands of live oak trees. Robledal is the essence of old Santa Barbara. It was built by the same artisans who built Santa Barbara's famous courthouse, the centerpiece of the city. Smith used the patterns made by the sunlight and shadows as a design element affecting line and proportion. At Robledal, the shifting sky, clouds, and foliage demand a purity of

form in the building. When designing his own house in 1916, he relied on impressions from a visit to Spain and the experiences he had while exploring the farmhouses of the Andalusian countryside. Smith believed that in art and architecture, heavily "refined" forms and "primitive" forms eventually became one.

The current owner bought the ranch in 1979 with his wife and young child. A designer, builder, and passionate devotee of George Washington Smith, he began to make a few modifications over time. A solarium was added in the center of the

ABOVE: Old oaks and narrow cypresses give the stone terrace, fountain, and gardens a suggestion of Moorish architecture.

OPPOSITE: Fences and pastures run through the coastal slopes to the Pacific Ocean.

OPPOSITE: The motor court reveals the variety of wrought-iron grates and the flourish of cacti and other plants.

UPPER RIGHT: Horses graze as the coastal fog moves up the slopes.

LOWER RIGHT: A beautiful drive under the old oaks leads to and from the ranch.

house to establish a source of natural light. He also designed and fabricated furniture for the dining room and a desk for his office, all in accordance with the proper proportions of the original architect.

One of the most inspirational of Smith's designs, in which he combined the landscape and the architecture, the Robledal Ranch is elegant and understated. Outside is the view of the Channel Islands in the Pacific, and inside is a composition of simple details. Lancet arches, basket arches, Moorish arches, and Gothic arches are all treated in white plaster of varied widths and heights. The effect produces the sensation of gliding between rooms and spaces, with subtle changes of light and shadows. Thick, pillow-cut, Saltillo tiles are found throughout the house in differing borders, designs, patterns, and spacing. Each riser on the stairs maintains its own design and color scheme. The main entry is a large, twenty-one-by-fourteen-foot foyer stepping down into the living room. With a strong, open-beamed ceiling and hand-carved braces, the living room features an iconic Smith white-plastered fireplace and mantel. Opposite the fireplace, the living room opens to a tiled loggia, with views of the ocean and the lower horse pasture. Horse trails run through the oaks for miles into the mountains or directly to the ocean's edge.

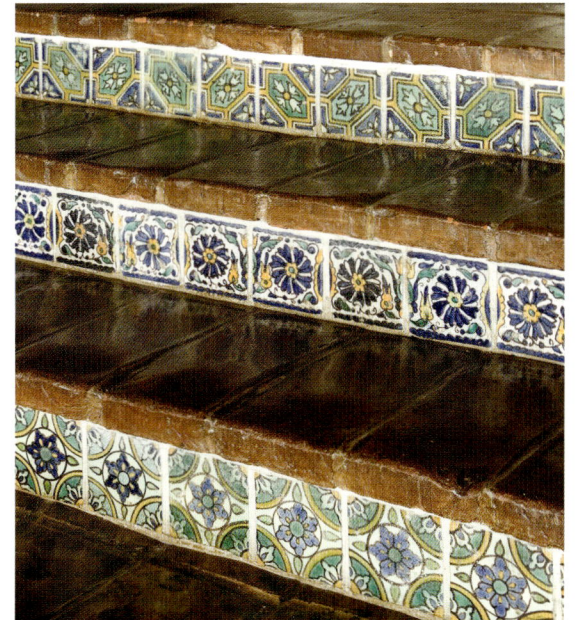

OPPOSITE: A view from the terrace through the foyer to the front entrance.

ABOVE: A sample of the many arch designs throughout the passages and thresholds.

ABOVE RIGHT: The foyer steps down to the main level, where stairs go to rooms above and a hallway leads to the living room.

LOWER RIGHT: A detail of painted tiles on the risers of the foyer steps.

LOWER LEFT: Strong details in the hand-carved ceiling brace.

OPPOSITE: A quintessential George Washington Smith fireplace angled in white plaster. The floor is clad in tile, and the wood ceiling is in a beamed and squared pattern. The view is to the ocean.

ABOVE: The combined detailing of the arched gate, the *vigas* ceiling, simple tiles in tight patterns, and the soft Moorish arches of the hall are all elements from the classical Spanish hacienda ranches.

RIGHT: A small window niche with a basket arch above. Spanish carved doors are on the right.

Vermejo Park Ranch, *New Mexico*

Vermejo Park ranch is located in the Sangre de Cristo mountain range of northern New Mexico and southern Colorado. Raton, New Mexico, is on the northeastern boundary of the ranch; Cimarron, New Mexico, is on the southeastern boundary; and the western boundary is on the crest of Stateline and Big Costilla peaks. The ranch is the heart of the historic two-million-acre Maxwell Land Grant created in 1841. The grant appears on all maps as the Beaubien-Miranda Grant. Charles Hypolite Beaubien, a French Canadian, was a trader with the Hudson Bay Company on an expedition that accidentally strayed into Mexico. Arrested and taken to Mexico City, he and his party were jailed briefly then released with permission to remain in New Mexico if they wished. Beaubien went to Taos, where he eventually became a prosperous trader. On January 8, 1841, Beaubien and his good friend, Guadaloupe Miranda, the secretary of the provisional government of Santa Fe, petitioned the governor for the lands that eventually became the Maxwell Land Grant. Nothing was done for two years, but in February 1843, Beaubien and Miranda asked a local justice of the peace to install them as the new owners of the site, which must have been somewhere near Cimarron. With five witnesses, the justice "took them by the hand, walked with

them, caused them to throw earth, pull up weeds, and show other evidences of possession."

Lucien B. Maxwell was a French-Canadian fur trapper who, with Kit Carson, served as a guide to explorer John Charles Fremont on his courageous western expeditions. Maxwell became friends with Beaubien and married his daughter, Luz. When Beaubien died in 1864, Maxwell and Luz began buying out the remaining heirs. By 1865 they were the sole owners of 1,714,765 acres, a territory roughly the size of Rhode Island.

Maxwell was a character to match the size of his empire. He loved gambling, drinking, and almost any extravagance. Physically powerful, he once took a bullet in the neck during an Apache ambush on the New Mexico–Colorado border and rode more than one hundred miles to the nearest doctor. The Maxwells built an immense Mexican-style home at Cimarron, with separate dining rooms for men and

OPPOSITE: A bird's-eye view of the Casa Grande and the main lodge and buildings of Vermejo Park.

ABOVE: Casa Grande stands against the backdrop of reddish hills.

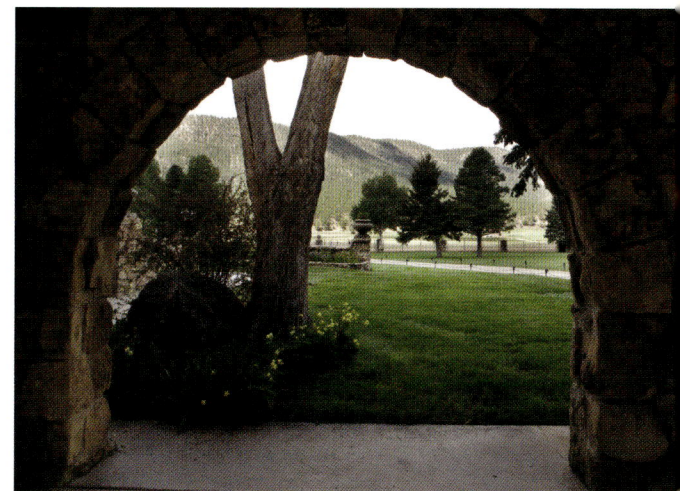

women; the men's eating area alone accommodated twenty. They built a billiards room, a gambling room, and a dance hall. The women were restricted to private quarters at the rear of the house. The home was a prominent stop on the Santa Fe Trail and a base for prospectors, hunters, and trappers. One guest wrote of the house, "The surroundings and whole atmosphere of the place reminded me of the descriptions that I had read of baronial estates in Europe in the Middle Ages." Maxwell was a generous landowner; however, ironically, his fortunes fell with the discovery of gold on this land in 1866. Around 1906 William H. Bartlett, a wealthy grain speculator from Chicago, purchased the land and began moving cattle there.

He also developed five lakes, stocking them well, and brought in elk, which had been nonexistent on the property.

Between 1907 and 1910 three elaborate stone residences and the greenhouses were built. The middle house, finished in 1908, was built around a large patio and contained many rooms for guests, a huge dining room, and a kitchen. Casa Grande was built especially for Bartlett, who by 1910 had given up his Chicago business interests and moved permanently to the ranch. He became an excellent horseman, an avid fisherman, and a benevolent employer who enjoyed life as a New Mexico cattleman. He was a beloved host, sportsman, and conservationist. Bartlett

LEFT: The facade of the Casa Grande bears a Mexican-style mission arch of stone.

ABOVE: Large brick kilns were built to burn coal.

RIGHT: Casa Grande at dawn. The large porches and arched loggias are lighted. The private quarters are on the far right, behind the arched windows on the main floor.

OPPOSITE: The grand central room was restored; the original glass-fronted bookcases were returned to border the walls of the room. The barrel-ceiling architecture and panels were painted and finished. Wood flooring was discovered under years of carpeting and restored. Natural light fills every space and the music room.

LEFT: Two lovely tufted banquettes in an inglenook, with windows flanking the fireplace, were fully restored.

RIGHT: A mirrored reflection of the bookcases and windows.

died suddenly in 1918, and within two years both his sons died, ending an era of Vermejo's history.

The land has since gone through several owners, most recently the Pennzoil Company, which purchased Vermejo in 1973 and sold it to Ted Turner in 1996. Vermejo is the largest of Mr. Turner's land holdings, at 590,823 acres. Elevations vary from 6,500 feet to mountains as high as 13,000 feet. Over 60 percent of Vermejo is southwestern ponderosa pine forest. Other tree species include bristlecone pine, piñon pine, aspen, juniper, oak, spruce, and Douglas and white firs.

When the property was purchased, Mr. Turner was married to Jane Fonda, who took on an enormous project with Casa Grande and several of the cottages on the ranch. Working with designers Barbara Pohlman and Robin Laughlin, she began a creative adventure to restore and improve the interiors of the buildings At that time Ms. Fonda believed the interior for Casa Grande should have, "more of a Teddy Roosevelt look." The efforts began with the discovery of dozens of treasures. Beautiful Italian mosaic tile was found under carpet in the entry, and hardwood flooring was uncovered in the living room. An elegant balcony above a dining area overlooking the first-floor library had been walled over. An extraordinary French limestone fireplace surround— a story and a half high and flanked by two tufted banquettes in an inglenook—was discovered; its mantle carvings, its arches, and a niche had been painted decades earlier. Leaded-glass–fronted bookcases were found stacked in a barn on the property.

Ms. Fonda worked from archival photographs, and her discoveries continued. The original balcony lamps are in use, as are the sconces. Original details such as doorknobs and nickel joints on the doors were also kept in use. The photos show that the architecture of the cottages was in the same motif as that of Casa Grande. The horse stables were in a medium-sized stone building with two Spanish-shaped gables, featuring a bull's-eye window in each and tiles on the roof. The cottages, which once housed the secretary, the doctor, the butler, and the men's quarters, each have a unique style, but all are made from the same stone with some stucco, and Spanish detailing in windows, facades, and roof styling.

The archival photos show that the original interiors of Casa Grande were very dark. The cantilevered arches of the library and the living room were made of solid oak rising from the bookcases in paneled walls. In the high barrel ceilings, inlaid panels divided the cavernous void. The entry staircase and wainscoting leading to the second floor were also oak. During the renovation the decision was made to paint out the dark wood, a bold move, but the soft colors and accents added life to the spaces. The interiors are stunning, the history of the architecture remains intact, and many original elements have been retrieved. The result is a supporting testament to the architectural vision of Vermejo.

OPPOSITE: The lovely small balcony was found hidden behind a wall. Many of the original lamps and sconces were discovered, along with other pieces to authenticate the work. Below, the dining room was revivified with pressed plants.

ABOVE: The staircase at the main entry. Its post, balusters, and railings were painted, as were the wainscoting panels on the walls.

RIGHT: The massive main door opens to reveal a stunning compass-style mosaic directional, which serves as a border and path to the adjoining rooms.

Turner has always had an interest in land and the natural world. He first sought properties for recreational use, specifically those with good hunting and fishing. He then began to acquire land to raise bison, and restore the landscape to its original condition. At Vermejo there is a strong focus on restoration and the enhancement of the ranch's many diverse ecosystems, ranging from the short grass prairie on the east side to the alpine tundra on the west side at elevations near 13,000 feet. There are no longer any cattle at Vermejo, only a population of twelve hundred free-ranging bison. Every winter the bison are worked through the corral, where calves and yearlings may be selected from the herd for placement at other ranches. Mr. Turner realized his fondness for the West and its beauty and wildlife when he bought his first ranch, the Bar None, in Montana in 1987. He has a genuine and powerful connection to the land and to nature.

ABOVE: This lovely stone-walled room with a stone arch window was originally an afternoon room.

RIGHT: A guest suite on the second floor.

San Antonio

S. Benito
S. Marietta

Visalia

Pt. Gorda

TULARE
LAKE

Tule R.

San Miguel

White R.

Key E.

Piedras Blancas
St. Simeon Harbor

St. Simons

R. Estada

Estrella

B   U   E   N   A   V   I   S

La Panza

Black Bar

Esteros

S   A   N   L   U   I   S

Estero Bay
Canada del Chow

S. Margarita

Carisa

Mt. Diablo

San Luis Obispo

THE PARK

O   B   I   S   P   O

San Luis Obispo

Kern L.

Pt. Sal.

Nipoma

Guayama R.

Buena Vista L.

R. Tejon

Mt. Diablo

Pt. Purisima

Alamico

Santa Inez

O de los Uvas Pass

Jesus Marice
Purissima

Los Pueblos

Pt. Arguilla
S. Julian
S. Cara

S. Inez

Pt. Tejon

San F

S   A   N   T   A   B   A   R   B   A   R   A

Point Conception

Santa Barbara

S. Cajetano

Santa Clara

Camula

San Buenaventura

Santa

Saticoy

Las Posa

CHANNEL OF SANTA BARBARA

San Miguel   Cuylers Harbor

Santa Rosa

Santa Cruz

Pt. Duma

Los Angeles
S.

San Ped

Pt. Vincent

Pt. Firmin

Catalina Harbor

Santa Catalina

San Nicolas

Capistrano

JOHNSON'S

Course of Mail Steamships

San Clemente

ALIFORNIA

TERRITORIES OF

EW MEXICO

Part VI: *Conclusion*

If it was a good house 150 years ago, it will be a good house today.

The French Ranch, *California*

Architect and builder John Winton Byers loved native California architecture, especially its Spanish and Mexican roots. His architectural compositions flowed with spontaneity and joy. The simplicity of the adobe arrangements was confounding, prompting one East Coast builder upon seeing the blueprints to comment, "Well, whaddayu know about that? Mud! Now that is interesting. But now tell me, between you 'nd I, d'you consider these particularly classy designs? Look so plain. Why, our farm hands in the old days built just that way without nobody ever calling it architecture." That comment took place in 1927, while a magazine editor was looking over a collection of photographs for a feature on new California residential architecture.

The French Ranch property was first purchased in the mid-1920s, when Major Leigh and Eleanor Brown French bought nearly three thousand acres of a Spanish land grant to raise cattle. The acreage was a few hours out of Los Angeles, nestled in the Santa Monica Mountains, intimately abutting twenty thousand acres of state and country lands in an area of uncertainty and isolation. A natural valley runs through the heart of it, with an ancient geologic fault that resulted in two very different rock formations. The north portion of the ranch bears soft, striated, flat beige sandstone, and the south portion consists of Topanga stone, which appears round and blue-molten-gray in color. Wildlife such as puma, red and gray fox, coyotes, and birds find their way through and across the land.

OPPOSITE: A view of the main house, with the owner's Brangus cattle approaching the "cow wall."

RIGHT: The motor court approach to the house around the fountain to the front gate.

Major French was a gentleman adventurer who rode with Teddy Roosevelt and the Rough Riders. The ranching life was an easy fit into his dauntless pursuits. His wife, much younger and a recent graduate of college in New York, thrived on the ranch experience. The couple commissioned John Byers to design and build their hacienda on the property in the mid- to late-1920s. Major French died young, and Mrs. French spent her many remaining years as a single woman working a cattle ranch. She raised Hereford cattle and became the much-admired grande dame of the region's cattle and farming community. Sadly, the Frenches were without heirs to their extraordinary ranch.

Today's owner purchased the French Ranch from the family trust when the stalwart Mrs. French passed away at the age of ninety-two. The ranch had not been touched since 1925; it was a piece of Old California, with no paved roads and the original cattle chutes and barns. This historic piece of architecture was a treasure. The owner is an enthusiast of architecture and what he has coined as the "Spanish colonial revival." This is a reference to the early 1800s Rancho period when Spain ruled Alta California and land was granted in large parcels upon petition to the ruling governor. Tragically, this unique and wonderful Byers relic was destroyed by fire in 1982, shortly after the owner bought the property.

Passion and commitment were the driving forces behind the determination to rebuild on the site, to maintain the original footprint of the residence and continue the work on the project in the same way

LEFT: The loggia runs the length of the house front.
ABOVE: A restored windmill and pump house.

BELOW: The John Byers Spanish- and Moorish-influenced tile and mosaic outdoor pool.

OPPOSITE: A newly purchased prize admired by local horsemen at the French Ranch, ca. 1925.

John Byers would have if he were alive today. The owner and architects documented the measurements and dimensions of the original house and began the re-creation and expansion on the same site. In the new design the main entry opens to the living room and library, with an adjoining gallery. Upstairs is a large master suite with dressing room and bath. A wing was added to each end of the original house, one housing the dining area and the opposite housing an office, creating a three-sided structure around a beautiful courtyard. There are three bedrooms downstairs, as well as an extraordinary vaulted, tiled kitchen of

LEFT: The center of the living area; above is a wrought-iron chandelier and two small windows. The ceiling is heavily beamed in the Spanish style. Spanish revival furniture collected from the Del Ray and Monterey collections furnishes the rooms.

BELOW: A passage under a hyperbolic parabola into the study. A deeply carved Spanish trunk offsets the large squared-timber and beam ceiling.

ABOVE: Stair risers decorated with custom-designed tile lead to an art and reading loft. The rails are custom wrought iron in a Spanish motif modeled after the original John Byers design. The arched opening is signature John Byers.

tremendous vision and daring. The tile came from California Pottery. The project took five and a half years and was quite complex. The owner's eye for detail required an intimate collaboration: three architects consulted on the project in separate phases.

The final phase was completed when the owner called in the firm of Michael Burch Architects, which specializes in Spanish colonial revival restoration and

design. Michael Burch and Diane Wilk came to the project to make their client's vision a reality. Burch was involved in almost all the myriad details required to finish the house. Integrated into the completion phase were modifications to drawings for nearly every room, tile specifications, hand-forged hardware, and Honduras mahogany and endless finish details. Room sizes were expanded to accommodate

the placement of precise custom-made tile designs, which were not to be modified. As the supervising architects, Burch and Wilk created such exterior details as the cow wall surrounding the courtyard and the wonderful freshwater fountains. Furnishings are from 1920s Monterey and Del Rey curated furniture collections. The individual bedrooms have period bedroom sets collected from the 1920s.

The owner's passion never diminished, and his vision never wavered. His love for the French Ranch, his land, and cattle is evident. He has preserved it to show us how to achieve a simple, yet elegant way to live in the twenty-first century. The result is a pristine reconstruction and restoration of a historic structure for the state of California.

ABOVE: The spacious dining room features exquisite custom floor tiles. Art consultant Debe Hale was responsible for the tile design and patterns throughout the restoration.

OPPOSITE: Masterful design and workmanship have turned this kitchen into a tile cathedral. Areas for preparation, cooking, and eating receive natural light from the doors to the terrace.

FAR LEFT: The master bedroom features a signature Byers fireplace design with a shallow tile hearth. French doors open to small balconies on each side of the room. A small door connects to the dressing room and bath.

LEFT: The owner's collection of art pottery and personal pieces.

BELOW: The restored bath is stunning in its beauty and the efforts to perfect it. The original fixtures were salvaged from a 1982 fire, restored, and polished. The 1920s California revival tiles are Moorish in design but Spanish in color.

Acknowledgments

Where is the West? I wasn't convinced that was a real question when I began this book. Dr. Walter Nugent of Notre Dame has done a survey of writers and editors to discover the parameters of the West. True, much can be speculated from studies, inventories, and reports. These have defined a place on a map called "The Unambiguous West," and it turns out that part of Colorado, part of Wyoming, half of Montana, all of Texas, and most of California are not included. Perhaps intellectual scrutiny is never enough; it does not get us even close to the West. The prominent philosopher Martha Nussbaum would recommend that passion, courage, and goodwill are the means by which knowledge is gained. These same ideals form the character of the West. And ranches are most certainly the heart of the matter. I thank the many wonderful and brave ranch owners that I met and spoke with during my research. I was told many stories, some of which could have happened eighty or ninety years ago but instead took place in the last few years. Being bold is a necessary part of the West.

I especially wish to thank Elena Cizmaric of TEI for her generosity, which I will always remember. My appreciation is extended to Lisa Newsom, founder and editor-in-chief of *Veranda* magazine, and Linda Rye, associate editor. I thank Diana Beattie for her energy and gracious willingness to provide expertise and resources at any time. I am particularly grateful to Marley + Wells Architects for allowing us to publish another of their fine projects and for their meticulous background material. I wish to thank architect Christopher Hill for our conversations and his willingness to keep digging. Also my appreciation goes to those who have a passion for history and architecture: Donald B. McDonald, Peter Pennoyer, Larry Pearson, Jonathan L. Foote, Kip Halvorsen of Faure Halvorsen, John Cottle of CCY, Kyle Tage of Locati Architects, and every architect who is strengthening and reinterpreting the quarterages of the West, those who restore them, and those who continue the work on projects that were begun a hundred years ago or more. Thank you.

To the photographers who participated in this book, I am grateful for your superb communication skills, initiative, and professionalism. It has been my good fortune and a great pleasure to work with you. I am grateful to many libraries and research staff, in particular, Kathryn Kanjo, museum director, and Jennifer Whitlock, project archivist of the Architecture & Design Collection, University Art Museum, University of California at Santa Barbara. My thanks to Nancy Clark, registrar at the Yellowstone Art Museum in Billings, Montana, for her help; Cynthia Hoff, interlibrary loan assistant, and Linda Maddux, reference librarian, Hauser Memorial Library, Reed College, Portland, Oregon; Margaret H. Bean, resource sharing librarian, Knight Library, University of Oregon, Eugene. Thank you to Charlene Walker, president, Lahaina Printsellers, Lahaina, Hawaii, for providing the A. Johnson territorial and state maps, circa 1860s. I also wish to thank Daniel Kosharek at the Palace of the Governors Photo Archives, New Mexico History Museum, Santa Fe. And thanks to Anne-Lise Wamstad of the Threshold Group, Suzanne Perking at Sotheby's, Stephen Downarovitz, and Pat Saraca for their expertise and assistance.

I want to thank my family and friends for their support: Dawna Galarneau Miller, for our Saturday morning breakfasts, and Bob Miller; my love to Richard, Genevieve, and Nicole Galarneau; my love to Timothy Paul and Michi Murayama; Tiffany Miller and Diane Abernathy, all for being a loving family. Thanks to Kerry D. Hampton III for his eternal friendship, and to Michael and Madeline Hampton. To Geraldine Foote-Fritts, thank you for the work you've done; your support and activism are an inspiration to everyone and more than a "step-up" for many people; my gratitude to Gregg and Nate Fritts. My thanks to Marilyn Booth-Love and Ken Love, whose charitable efforts are immeasurable. I would like to thank, in memoriam, my stepmother, Christine Connolly Galarneau Kinney, for her lifelong inspiration and guidance. And my gratitude and love, in memoriam, to Enid Thompson Sales, for her friendship, humor, and scholarship, and for introducing me to Carmel, California. My greatest love to Malcolm and Murphy.

It is always an honor to work with Mr. Charles Miers, publisher of Rizzoli. This book is for him. I thank you, Charles, and am grateful to you for giving me this spectacular project. To my editor, Alexandra Tart, who never fails to teach me something new about the work I do. I am so appreciative to you Alex, for your patience, composure, and unfailing guidance. It is a gift to have you on my side. I also have the good fortune to work with Lynne Yeamans and admire her art as our book designer. You've been wonderful, Lynne. I thank Rizzoli publicity director Pam Sommers and her staff for efforts on my behalf.

For Robert: you are a dream of patience and wonder, and as Cormac does, you are so funny you make yourself laugh. I love you laughing.